Recons

Other titles by Anne Borrowdale:

A Woman's Work: Changing Christian Attitudes
(SPCK 1989)

*Distorted Images: Christian Attitudes to Women, Men
and Sex* (SPCK 1991)

Reconstructing Family Values

Anne Borrowdale

First published in Great Britain 1994
Society for Promoting Christian Knowledge
Holy Trinity Church
Marylebone Road
London NW1 4DU

British Library Cataloguing-in-Publication Data
A catalogue record for this book is available from the British Library

ISBN 0-281-04762-6

Typeset by Anne Borrowdale   _2002756_
Printed in Great Britain by
The Cromwell Press,
Melksham, Wiltshire

For Derrick, Pat,
Jan, Chris, and Tim

Contents

Introduction

If there was one thing everyone seemed to agree on in the early months of 1993, it was that Britain was a nation in crisis. Family life had broken down, crime was soaring, children were out of control, and there was no consensus of morality or faith by which to live. Fears about the erosion of 'family values' had been around for some years, and there had been intermittent interest in the media – particularly in relation to juvenile crime and the rise in the numbers of single parents. But what focused the concern, was the dreadful killing by two children of two-year-old James Bulger. Paradoxically, at the same time as a wave of sympathy, concern, and moral outrage swept the country, the event was seen as a symbol of Britain as a nation devoid of morality and caring. It brought a tide of articles and editorial comment lamenting the moral state of the nation in general, and the nation's children in particular. 'Something has gone dreadfully wrong with Britain', argued psychology professor Richard Lynn in the *Daily Mail*: 'We have become a helpless society, helpless to confront the crime which makes life a misery in so many parts of our country, helpless to maintain standards of decency, helpless to reverse the trend.'[1] A *Daily Mirror* editorial similarly asserted: 'There is something rotten at the heart of Britain. A creeping evil of violence and fear.'

Agreed about the nature of the crisis, people searched about for something or somebody to blame. Some went for sheer human wickedness, with one writer in *The Times* commenting, 'Some children are born bad.' There was a tendency to demonize the young: angels when victims, but monsters when they offended.

1

Others blamed parents or the lack of parents, schools, and the permissive, Left-wing liberals they claimed had dominated teacher-training or childcare advice from the 1960s onwards. Those at opposite ends of the political spectrum accused one another. As Melanie Phillips had noted eighteen months earlier, the political debate gets mainly premised upon blame: 'The right blames the left for a climate of permissiveness that has created single parents, substituted selfishness for discipline and inflicted a rising tide of social misery upon the nation. The left blames the right for creating poverty and inequality and says the difficulties facing families are all the government's fault because it has kicked away their props.' The Right rails at personal selfishness in divorcees and working mothers, she says, but 'their political creed extols self-interest and individuals doing their own thing while denigrating collective responsibility'. The Left fails to recognize that 'their strong political sense of a collective social ethic runs directly counter to their attachment to anything-goes personal relationships, to undiluted individualism in family structures'.[2]

Also implicated in their turn were television, advertising, feminism, diet, the government, the Church, the decline in Sunday School membership, and society in general – 'we are all to blame for James's death', said the Bishop of Liverpool, David Sheppard.[3] All of these things can be said to have contributed to a greater or lesser degree to the culture in which children are growing up today. However, blaming one or more of these influences for a moral breakdown in society is far too simplistic, and obscures the fact that such things often have good sides as well as sometimes creating problems.

Though concern about families, crime, and values continued to be aired from time to time, the intensity of the moral panic passed, as these things do. The trial and sentencing of James Bulger's murderers in December 1993, received massive media coverage, but did not give rise to the same degree of national soul-searching. The focus was on the 'unparalleled evil' in the hearts of two individual boys rather than on a sick society, although video violence did get mentioned as a contributory cause.

What was missing in most people's analysis at the height of the moral panic was any sense of history, the fact that we had been here before. Cohen described in 1972 how from time to time societies are subject to periods of moral panic:

> A condition, episode, person or group of persons emerges to become defined as a threat to societal values and interests; its nature is presented in a stylized and stereo-typical fashion by the mass media; the moral barricades are manned by editors, bishops, politicians and other right-thinking people; socially accredited experts pronounce their diagnoses and solutions; ways of coping are evolved or [more often] resorted to; the condition then disappears . . . or deteriorates. [4]

Such moral panics have occurred in Britain in just about every decade since the 1930s, and the parallels in the language used of these perceived crises is strikingly similar. Attention is focused particularly on juvenile crime, and 'a crisis of authority, pivoting around youth, the family and moral conduct'.[5] This is not to deny that juvenile crime, family, and morality are serious concerns, and I shall return to them later. But a moral panic distorts the issues, and the steady stream of detailed work being done is passed over in favour of simplistic solutions. Moral panics tend to bounce politicians into hasty action and prevent them from seeking long-term solutions to what are actually complex problems. Because the Church finds itself in demand to help 'man the barricades', it tends to accept the prevailing analysis, and its contribution becomes irrelevant as public attention moves on.

A moral panic is triggered by a particular event or set of events, but there need to be other conditions for it to take hold in a nation's consciousness. Rising crime and family breakdown were significant current concerns in early 1993, but they had been around for some years. James Bulger's death was tragic, but such things have happened in the past; admittedly it is very rare, but children have committed murder before. Such events are not generally seen as reflections of what the *nation* has become. It was as if this particular event acted as a lightning conductor, channelling very real anxieties about crime and family breakdown, and perhaps about social change in general.

The moral panic of early 1993 also arose during a period of great social change. The Conservative Party had spent thirteen and a half years changing the face of welfare provision, employment, and education. Serious issues were being raised about national identity in relation to the European community, and both the monarchy and the Church of England were facing critical internal problems. Such things do not necessarily matter to people individually, but the debate about them contributes to a sense that the old established values no longer hold. Among Christians, questioning about articles of faith and ministry had created uncertainty. It is not surprising that people at such times look back to a mythical golden age when all was well, and call for 'traditional values'. Also perhaps, *one* toddler's death was a horror which could be grasped. As 1992 merged into 1993, nightly television images of children's suffering in former Yugoslavia and Somalia were relentless. Powerless to do anything very much about these manifestations of human greed and hatred, and disturbed by change even if it was good, perhaps it was natural that people should focus so much attention on a single tragedy where explanations were easy to come by, and there could be clear candidates for blame.

Unfortunately it isn't possible to find single, simple answers to questions about why we have the kind of society we do; we need a much more thorough analysis. This book did not start out as an attempt to address such questions – it was originally intended to be a general book about the family from a Christian perspective. But it was the subject of values which came to interest me most, and the debate which took place early in 1993 provided a lot of material. Indeed, a few months after the instant moralizing had died down, some thoughtful television programmes were screened that examined young offenders, children's values, and family life, and I have drawn on some of these. It continues to be necessary to ask what values are important for families, and what is meant by the demand for a return to 'family values' in society. We need to ask about the role of the Christian community in society – are we the moral guardians of the nation or something more unassuming? And how do we treat children, as a society, as parents (if we have children), and as adults living with the child within ourselves?

The subject of family life can be a fraught one, yet it is an essential one for all of us. We may be parents ourselves, and

4

feelings about that experience vary widely. Even if we do not have children of our own, most of us will relate to other people's offspring in some way – perhaps through our jobs, or simply because we can't help tripping over them in supermarkets. And we have all once been children, growing up either within families, or with adults who acted as parents to us. Many of us will continue to have contact with our family of origin, and still be working through tensions in those relationships. Adult children may find themselves caring for frail parents.[6] Family relationships are supportive for many people, yet some are still living painfully with a legacy of abuse from their childhood.

There are several reasons why it needs to be part of the theological agenda to look at how people come to terms with the influence of their parents, and what legacy we leave if we are parents ourselves. Firstly, it is a matter of pastoral concern to examine how the hurts of childhood can be healed and prevented. It is true that most children survive what happens to them, and learn to live with the scars. But it is worth challenging negative patterns in family life, not only because the destructive attitudes they foster are so common in wider life, but because children are people who matter. The Christian Church does not have a good track record when it comes to looking at children as grow- ing people rather than converts for the future. Christians have campaigned in large numbers for the right to life of the unborn child, but our practices and theology have all too often made it clear that we are not much interested in the right to full life for the *born* child. Secondly, we need to recognize that what goes on within families has repercussions for wider society. It is not that all the ills of society can be laid at the door of poor parenting – for social policy, education, and circumstance also have a part to play. But upbringing is one factor that needs to be addressed. Thirdly, there are specific questions that theologians need to ask about the values and theological themes which underlie what happens in domestic relationships, and that is a particular theme of this book.

There are many different approaches to the subject of families, and Christian perspectives have been offered on most of them. Yet the impression given is of a fragmented literature. Books on the family are often about family structure, and do not connect with the way ordinary people seek to make things work. Discussions of childrearing may be very practical, or concentrate on psychological insights, yet not connect with 'The Family' as an institution, or with the influence of social policy. (Throughout this book, I write the term 'The Family' when I am referring to institutional and symbolic understandings of it.) Philosophical discourse on the rights of children shows little appreciation of what children are really like. There are increasing numbers of 'pop psychology' books on the market which advise adults on how to overcome the consequences of their parents' failings – but they rarely consider the legacy which these same adults will bequeath to *their* children. Theological contributions to the debate seem most interested in family form, and popular Christian literature tends to have a rather·simplistic approach to the Bible as a guide for family living today. I have examined some of this material, because it has a wide readership among Christians. Sadly, it is striking how often what is said to be the Christian approach to families, 'God's way', is criticized in the secular literature as causing great damage to children and the adults they become. This is especially true of issues of discipline and obedience, as I shall show. The Church gets called on to uphold family values, but whether we really know more about them than anyone else is open to question. None the less, I think there are contributions we can make if we bring the wider themes of the gospel to bear on families, and there are helpful values we can stress.

It is impossible to do justice to all the different themes outlined above, but in what follows I have tried to draw on a wide range of different perspectives, and to see how they inform one another. If this book can suggest some fresh ideas for those involved in different disciplines, such as education, psychology, feminist theology, and so on, it will have achieved one of its purposes. My hope is that specialists in such areas will develop the detailed analysis which is beyond the scope of this book. Similarly, those whose roots are in other cultures will be better placed than I to examine whether the values I focus on make sense in their situation. The immediate context of this book is British society, though I do make some reference to the rest of Europe, and use quite a lot of material from the United States. However, a truly global perspective is not possible here, and indeed, given the variety of cultures and family experience, it would not be feasible to keep them all in view at the same time. I have done some research into different family experiences in minority ethnic groups in Britain, but am conscious of how much more remains to be done if there is to be proper dialogue about family values across the different communities in this country.

I have been very conscious of the limitations of writing from where I sit. I have read, and discussed the issues as widely as possible, in different parts of the country and with people from many walks of life, both inside and outside the Church. I live in a multicultural area, and mix with both children and parents from a variety of backgrounds through the local schools my children attend and through my work. This has expanded my horizons; but the fact remains that being brought up in a particular way in a white, middle-class family, and living as I do in a first marriage with a husband and two dependent children, influences my attitude to families.

I have had numerous discussions with people and groups on the subjects in this book, and cannot thank them all individually for their help. However, I would like to thank Barbara Hayes, Judith and Peter Judd, Frances Killick, Keith Lamdin, Jan Payne and Wendy Robinson for their helpful comments on the manuscript. Also, I acknowledge my debt to my fellow members on the General Synod Board for Social Responsibility Working Party on the Family, which began meeting in 1992, for stimulating discussions and help in locating material. This book does of course represent my personal views, and not those of the Working Party, or the others named, and any faults in the final product are entirely my own responsibility.

My thanks are also due to the Bishop of Oxford and the Oxford Diocesan Board for Social Responsibility for giving me three months' leave in 1993 in order to complete this book.

Notes

1. Unless otherwise attributed, quotations from newspapers are from P. Handley, 'Someone to Blame', *Church Times*, 26 February 1993, or from a project studying moral values in the *Sunday Express* and *Daily Express*, carried out by Pat Gilham for the Oxford Ministry course, March 1993.

2. M. Phillips, in M. Phillips, ed., *The Parent Trap* (Guardian Studies, vol. 4, 1991), p. 36.

3. This remark was criticized in the press. As Paul Handley noted in the *Church Times*, the 'apparent self-loathing in the sentiment "what have we all come to?" . . . means "what have we come to" to let *them* get away with this?'

4. S. Cohen, quoted in S. Hall et al., *Policing the Crisis* (London, Macmillan, 1978), p. 15.

5. Hall et al., *Policing the Crisis*, p. 305.

6. It is interesting that we have no word which distinguishes adult offspring from dependent children. I try to make it clear which group I am referring to. I generally speak of children and parents in the plural; this is because I am referring to many families, not because I am assuming that all children have siblings and two parents.

chapter one

Troublous Times

Children have bad manners and contempt for authority, they no longer rise when elders enter the room. They contradict their parents, chatter before company, gobble up their food and tyrannize their teachers.

<u>Aristotle 322 BC</u>[1]

The world is passing through troublous times. The young people of today think of nothing but themselves. They have no reverence for parents or old age. They are impatient of all restraint.

<u>Peter the Hermit 1050-1115</u>[2]

Looked at in his worst light the adolescent can take on an alarming aspect: he has learned no definite moral standards from his parents, is contemptuous of the law, easily bored . . . vulnerable to the influence of TV programmes of a deplorably low standard.

<u>British Medical Association 1961</u>[3]

The 'crisis in the family' gets spoken of as both cause and effect of a moral decline in Britain as a whole. What, though, is the actual evidence for moral decline? Family patterns have changed, as I shall discuss in Chapter 3, but how troublous in reality are the times we live in? This chapter cannot present a full report on the state of the nation, but I would like to look at some of the areas most commonly linked to a 'crisis in family values'.

Those who believe that Britain is facing a moral crisis have much evidence which they can cite. Statistics show that crime has gone up ninefold since 1950, and the British Crime Survey shows many more offences being committed than are recorded by the police.[4] Every week another brutal assault on an elderly person, woman, or child seems to hit the headlines. There is a growing number of racist attacks. Teachers, nurses, and social workers are increasingly subject to assaults. Britain's rate of family breakdown is one of the highest in Europe, and though the divorce rate is slowing down, it may only be because couples are less likely to get married in the first place. Increasing numbers of children are born outside marriage, and the number of one-parent families has been growing steadily. The boundaries of acceptability for violence, swearing, and sex on television have widened, and children can now have access to violent and pornographic material on video or computer games. And people's observations of daily life seem to confirm their sense that things are out of control: gangs of youths blocking the pavements, petty vandalism such as breaking newly planted trees or damaging a children's play area or being sworn at by young children.

That picture is a compelling interpretation of society as it now is, and I have heard it time and time again as I have talked with people. Yet it doesn't tell the whole story. Changing patterns of family life are not necessarily evidence of a moral crisis, as I shall point out. The majority of children still get 'good enough' parenting in reasonably stable family situations. There is still much evidence of people's capacity to care – the quantities of floral tributes placed at the spot where a child or adult has been killed surely reflect the heart of Britain more than the act of murder itself? We should remember too the amount of sacrificial caring that goes on in people's homes. At the last count, some 14 per cent of adults in the United Kingdom were officially carers, looking after an elderly or disabled person. It may not always be done well, for the caring role can create great strain, and 'elder abuse' may occur. But millions of people are still willing to take on caring responsibilities, and on top of that individuals are undertaking many other sorts of care – for example, dropping in

10

on an elderly neighbour or relative to prepare their daily meals. Caring community life does still exist.

Television is not all bad news either. It may show us violence as entertainment, but it also helps us to know more about the world we live in, and encourages generosity. The growth of violent pornography is worrying, but we might also point to a growth of concern for the environment among young people, and the way 'green' issues have become mainstream after decades of being seen as merely an eccentric hobby. Some young people may vandalize at will, but others are hard-working and helpful members of society. The increase in crime is very difficult to interpret, since statistics show what the police record, rather than the extent of crime, and police practice and the willingness of people to report offences alters from year to year. There is a lot of crime, and perceptions of it are high partly because it is touching new groups of people. The 1991 figures showed that crime was rising in mainly rural areas, but falling in other places. Some 94 per cent of crimes are crimes against property, which are indeed distressing, but the likelihood of being a victim of violence is still low.

It may be true that there are particular areas of our inner cities where order and law have broken down, but there are also plenty of decent people in such areas who don't like what is going on. Moss Side in Manchester is notorious for violence and drug-dealing, but residents there organized a march to show the opposition of the majority to what was happening in their neighbourhood. Easterhouse in Glasgow has been cited as an area where a feckless underclass rules, but as Bob Holman shows, there is a great deal of good family and community life there. Beatrix Campbell paints a depressing picture of life in 'Britain's dangerous places', yet she also points to community solidarity and action.[5]

Dealing with crime

Much has been said about the need for severe measures to be taken against persistent young offenders, and the impression given is of huge numbers of irredeemable delinquents. The levels of

11

petty nuisance and vandalism are high, but one police officer put the number of persistent juvenile offenders across the country at around 300 only. About 5 per cent of young offenders commit 70 per cent of the crime for their age group.[6] We tend to notice the actions of an antisocial minority and judge the majority by them. Though many youngsters, especially males, break the law to some degree, and a small minority commit horrific and violent crimes, most go on to settle down and lead normal lives. A third of all men born in the early 1950s had a conviction by the age of thirty-one. Yet if the lawless past of so many men currently in their forties is not seen as a major social problem, should we worry quite so much about the activities of today's teenagers? Will they too eventually settle down?[7] It is because this is recognized by many within the criminal justice system that so much effort has been put into keeping youngsters out of prison. Clearly, persistent, serious juvenile offenders need dealing with, and there are tried and tested forms of treatment which have a chance of changing their behaviour, and these need to be persevered with.

Unfortunately, though, the emphasis on severe punishment which develops at times of perceived moral crisis, works against such solutions. There have been recent cutbacks in special educational units which deal with youngsters who are truanting or disruptive in school, despite the fact that competition between schools means that difficult pupils are being excluded with increasing frequency. At a time when there is such concern about antisocial behaviour amongst the nation's youth, this seems to be short-sighted to say the least, for where will these children go, and who will help them to gain some control over themselves and their lives?[8] Demonizing young delinquents only sets them further apart from the rest of society. One government campaign against car thieves used the image of them as scavenging hyenas – an image more likely to encourage such thieves to prey on society, rather than shame them into good behaviour.

The evidence of things such as increased vandalism is often taken as an indication of declining moral standards peculiar to our own day, yet this behaviour has been going on from time immemorial. In every generation, adults have been critical of the youth of their day – as the quotations at the beginning of this chapter illustrate. Childhood has meant very different things through the ages, but the reactions of adults to young people have uncanny parallels with our own day. It is therefore difficult to know how much our sense that children are out of control is based on reality, and how much it reflects the usual adult perception of young people. How many of those of us who look critically at young people terrified our elders when we were that age, with our strange clothes and boisterous behaviour? We look back at our youth with nostalgia, and create a myth that back in the past, young people always respected their elders, and behaved well. We forget about the teddy boys in the 1950s, the fights between Mods and Rockers in the 1960s, the skinheads and football hooligans of the 1970s and 1980s. And today's older generation have forgotten that in the 1930s and 1940s there was great anxiety about a rise in juvenile crime, and accusations that 'the sense of parental responsibility has notoriously declined'.[9] Yet further back, there was an epidemic of street crime in the nineteenth century: 'Once more the streets of London are unsafe by day or night', said Cornhill Magazine in 1863.[10] Brake and Hale note that the first police officers were not universally accepted, and that working-class communities have had a long history of conflict with the police.

However, there do seem to be aspects of the current age which are worse than in the past – for example, drug-related crime and the use of weapons are both increasing. But clearly, there has never been a golden age when society was free of crime and everyone did as they were told. There have always been families, individuals, and groups who are violent, antisocial, and uncaring. Yet oddly, to say this appears to diminish the seriousness of the crime and violence we live with now, perhaps because 'we've seen it all before' is a classic way of detracting from the importance of some event or idea. And it seems that the choice is polarized – so that either one must hold that everything is in decline from former times, or that all is well, even improving. Utopia is thought to lie either in the past or in the future, but either way to be attainable. These two positions have some correlation with Right- and Left-wing political views, but not exclusively so.

Christians can be found in both these camps, and yet I think a more truly Christian perspective takes a difficult middle line which accepts that the world we live in is often depressing and brutal, but that *this always has been and always will be the case.* We were thrown out of Eden a long time ago. The *Church Times* editorial after James Bulger's death pointed out that one of the contributions Christians can make is to remind us that human wickedness exists, and that

> stories of past golden ages of behaviour are certainly untrue: the quotient of human wickedness has always been a constant: if criminals were once less rife than now, or children better behaved, it will in great part have been because the wielders of power over them were crueller. . . . human nature is intractable. Nowhere have its bad impulses been satisfactorily managed in the past, and nowhere will they be in the future. Truthful policy-making has to start from that melancholy point.[11]

The Christian task is to continue to work for what is good and right, without the guarantee of ultimate success. I have found Vaclav Havel's expression of this encouraging: 'Anyone who claims that I am a dreamer who expects to transform hell into heaven is wrong', he writes. 'I have few illusions. But I feel a responsibility to work towards the things I consider good and right. I don't know whether I'll be able to change certain things for the better, or not at all. Both outcomes are possible. There is only one thing I will not concede: that it might be meaningless to strive in a good cause.'[12] At a time of concern about moral decline, it is difficult to keep realism, faith, and hope in together, but this is one element of the Church's task.

Masculinity, crime, and violence

History teaches us that there has always been a significant group of young males whose behaviour ranges from annoyingly boisterous to downright criminal. Our culture shares with many other industrialized nations the problem of knowing how to guide its boys into adulthood, and how to deal with offending behaviour so as to prevent it becoming a way of life. It is difficult to judge whether there are proportionately more young men who are antisocial than there have ever been, or whether they are simply more visible, and their actions more costly in today's society. It has been suggested that some people, mainly males, have a predisposition towards aggression and violence, which gets triggered by upbringing or circumstance. This would not mean that males are born to be deviant, but that some of them will be more vulnerable to negative influences, within their families or in the world at large. If this is so, it would make sense to be careful about the culture in which boys are brought up, and not to reinforce their destructive tendencies at the expense of their caring ones. Boys may well be more prone to rough-and-tumble fighting, and be drawn towards violent toys, but this does not mean that parents should give up, sighing that 'boys will be boys'. For boys have many facets to their personalities, and they can be encouraged to be social and civilized.

Unfortunately, most of the entertainment and toys marketed at boys focuses on violence of one sort or another. And though there is no simple causal link between this and antisocial behaviour, it does seem odd that we complain about the level of violence in society, yet are happy to let boys entertain themselves with a culture of violence. Of course, it is true that children in the past have seen violence, heard violent stories in fairy tales, and played at war, but today's situation is substantially different. Children can now spend many hours each day surrounded by toys, television, videos, computer games, and music, all of which may have a violent content, and this is less often balanced by other activities and values.[13]

Whether we now live in a society which is more likely to trigger aggressive behaviour in those who are susceptible is hard to say. If antisocial behaviour is more prevalent, it may be that there are more people today than in previous years who feel they have no stake in society – and that this is a denial of their rights. Geoffrey Pearson may be right when he suggests in his book *Hooligan* that Britain has consistently failed to win the consent of substantial proportions of its people and to find a secure and trusting place in the social fabric for its youth.[14]

Ted Wragg makes the interesting point that the age at which children reach physical maturity has gone down since the mid-nineteenth century, whilst the school leaving age has gone up:

'Thus, whereas 100 years ago pupils left school before the age of 12 and were physically children for the first four or five years of their working life, today most stay in education until they are at least 17, especially with the spread of youth training schemes which effectively raised the school-leaving age by another year, yet they may have been physically, if not emotionally, young adults for some time.' If adolescent boys are more likely to be aggressive when they are reaching physical maturity, this period may be harder to manage now than it was when they were out in full-time work. Wragg concludes that 'A society leaves its adolescent males underemployed at its peril.'[15] However, full employment is no panacea for social ills when many in society feel alienated from it. Even young men who have regular jobs can cause trouble – the 1980s saw the rise of the 'lager lout', who was employed, and had money and aggression to burn.

An underclass?

Those on the political Left often point to unemployment or poverty as the cause of crime, but this is too simplistic. There does appear to be a link between inequality and crime – the wider the gap between rich and poor in a society, the more sharply crime increases. But neither inequality in society nor economic deprivation predicts whether an individual will be delinquent or not.[16] Whilst economic deprivation is a factor in delinquency, it is the way parents manage children which seems to dictate whether a harsh environment will lead to delinquency or not,[17] and I shall return to this point. If those on the political Left are too simplistic in seeing unemployment or poverty as the cause of crime, those on the political Right also offer a flawed argument in suggesting that both crime and unemployment are simply matters of young men making deliberately immoral choices. Right-wing commentators, notably Charles Murray, attribute social malaise to the growth of an underclass who are parasites on the state. This underclass consists of unemployed young men who choose not to take jobs, and instead turn to crime and drugs; and single mothers who choose to have children outside stable relationships, and whose offspring are delinquent and eventually become the next generation of criminals. These 'barbarians' (Murray's term) are seen as a dangerous threat to society, making unemployment and crime acceptable, destroying the model of the two-parent family, creating poverty, and encouraging fecklessness.

There have been a number of substantial critiques of this analysis. Kirk Mann argues against Murray that the middle classes cost the Treasury more with mortgage interest relief, company cars, and so on, but welfare is supposed only to corrupt the poor, not the corporate executive.[18] Bob Holman points out that whilst there are some wild children in Easterhouse, and crime exists, 72 per cent of children there live in two-parent families. The single mothers usually marry or cohabit again, and are not a permanent class. Those who are unemployed and claiming benefits are often very family oriented, and highly motivated to find jobs. The majority of males in Easterhouse are in employment, though it tends to be low-paid, part-time, or they are on work-schemes. While some people are so battered by circumstance that they show different behaviour, argues Holman, there is not a distinct breed of underclass in Easterhouse or anywhere else who have a different set of values from the rest of society.[19] Those on the Right would like to withdraw benefits from people they regard as the underclass, and some even suggest removing their right to vote. The idea is that these people would not choose to be unemployed or single parents if the state didn't support them, although there is scant evidence for this view.

The evils the Right complain of flourished in the Victorian era when there was very little welfare provision. Holman argues that the harsh, judgemental attitude towards unemployed men and single mothers, taken up by those who never seem to talk to those they pontificate about, is far from Christian. Once again, there is an emphasis here on exerting social control through punitiveness. The premise behind such ideas is flawed, however, because it rests on the assumption that human beings are free to make considered, rational choices. The reality is that the human condition is as described by St. Paul: unable to do what we want to do, and doing what we do not want to do, bound both by external pressures and our internal processes. As Brian Wren puts it:

We come with self-inflicted pains
Of broken trust and chosen wrong,
Half-free, half-bound by inner chains,

By social forces swept along,
By powers and systems close confined,
Yet seeking hope for humankind.[20]

The notion of an underclass is a useful one politically. It identifies a particular group that can be blamed, asserts that its members behave as they do because they have made a free choice to be immoral, and thus ensures that it is nothing to do with the rest of us. And, of course, if problems are the result of people's individual immorality, there is nothing much the state can do, and it certainly doesn't need to spend any money improving social conditions. Yet the environment can be powerful in giving the message that young people are not valued. Schools and neighbourhood facilities may be doing a good job, yet they are likely to be underfunded, poorly maintained, and have a bad reputation. Melanie Phillips, writing after riots in several cities in 1991, commented on this, and concluded:

> Faced with such huge cultural pressures, such alienation, such cynicism, such fragmentation of family and community, how difficult it is for parents to give their children that sense of the intrinsic value of their communities and of themselves. And how hypocritical of politicians of left or right to . . . [ignore] the part they themselves have played in presiding down the decades over a spiritually and intellectually arid culture that disenfranchises and excludes.[21]

The idea that people sin, and that therefore their behaviour at times needs to be restricted, is fair enough; but the emphasis on control through fear, shame, and punitiveness does not create a society at ease with itself. Believing that people also have good in them, and that this can be fostered, offers a more creative way forward, as it does with growing children. The same could be said of the need to work alongside other groups in society, when reform is being attempted. Many of those who in the past were regarded as symbols of authority – teachers, doctors, and even the police – have themselves been treated with very little respect by politicians and sections of the press. Attacks on members of such professions for resisting change have not only damaged their morale, but have undermined their authority. Bishops are called on to give a moral lead, yet are ridiculed and attacked. Constructive criticism and change are necessary, but the tactics seem to have been less those of consulting in order to move forward together, than of slapping down on any dissent and being disparaging about the resultant frustration.

This kind of behaviour, whether intentional or not, has echoes with that of an authoritarian parent who thinks children should do as they are told. That the 'children' in this case know themselves to be responsible adults has added to the sense of injustice many of them feel about how change has been handled. We are seeing 'family values' of a sort at the heart of national life, but they are not creating the sort of 'family' in which all the members can thrive.[22]

Notes

1. I cannot trace the source of this.

2. Quoted in *All God's Children* (London, National Society/Church House Publishing, 1991), p. 28.

3. Quoted in M. Phillips, ed., *The Parent Trap* (Guardian Studies, Vol. 4, 1991), p. 19.

4. Statistics used in this book are taken from various sources, and I do not give specific references for each one. Sources used are the *General Household Survey* (London, HMSO, 1992); *Social Trends* (London, HMSO, 1993 and 1994); D. Dormer, *The Relationship Revolution* (London, One Plus One, 1992); Family Policy Studies Centre Fact Sheets; and a course on families run through Oxford University Department of Continuing Education, January–March 1993. Statistics are, of course, subject to interpretation and revision. However, the information referred to here should give a general picture of what is happening in relation to families.

5. B. Holman, 'The Underclass: A Christian Response', *Third Way*, March 1993; B. Campbell, *Goliath* (London, Methuen, 1993). Though Campbell tends to overstate a division between noble women and feckless men, and has been criticized for not representing the communities entirely accurately, the book does convey the strengths as well as the distress of people living in troubled communities.

6. Spt Russ Horne, at a conference organized by the charity Exploring Parenthood, 1992.

7. It could be argued that it is these lawless men who are the inadequate fathers of today's tearaways, of course, but although

having a criminal parent is a factor in children's delinquency, there does not seem to be an exact correlation.

8. These themes are explored in D. Utting, J. Bright, and C. Henricson, *Crime and the Family* (London, Family Policy Studies Centre, 1993).

9. E. Smithies, *Crime in Wartime* (London, George Allen & Unwin, 1982), p. 173.

10. Quoted in Hall et al., *Policing the Crisis* (London, Macmillan, 1978), p. ix. This book, together with *Crime in Wartime*, and M. Brake and C. Hale, *Public Order and Private Lives* (London, Routledge, 1992), provide an important corrective to the usual view of previous decades as times of law, order, and social stability. These publications also show that floggings and harsh sentencing policies did not halt the rise in crime.

11. *Church Times*, 26 February 1993.

12. Quoted in the 'Strasbourg Briefing' from the Anglican Representative at the European Institutions, 1992.

13. For a lengthy discussion of these issues in a North American context, see M. Miedzian, *Boys will be Boys* (London, Virago, 1993). Also see A. Phillips, *The Trouble with Boys* (London, Pandora, 1993).

14. Quoted in M. Phillips, 'Alienation Runs Riot', *The Guardian*, 13 September 1991.

15. T. Wragg, 'Education for the Twenty-first Century', in *Alternative Educational Futures*, ed. C. Harber et al. (New York, Holt, 1984).

16. C. Pond, 'Crime, Poverty, Inequality', *Equalities News*, November 1993, No. 18. p.7.

17. See Utting et al., *Crime and the Family*.

18. K. Mann, *The Making of an English Underclass* (Milton Keynes, Open University Press, 1992).

19. Holman, 'The Underclass'.

20. B. Wren, 'Great God, your love has called us here'.

21. M. Phillips, *Guardian*, 13 September 1991.

22. The link between parent and state, or the 'Nanny State' as some call it, is problematic. This, as I shall argue later, is partly because it is based on an unhelpful philosophy of parenting.

chapter two

Values in a
Changing Society

A ragged urchin, aimless and alone,
Loitered about that vacancy, a bird
Flew up to safety from his well-aimed stone:
That girls are raped, that two boys knife a third,
Were axioms to him, who'd never heard
Of any world where promises were kept.
Or one could weep because another wept.

W. H. Auden[1]

The last chapter focused on the sense that something has gone
seriously wrong in Britain, a feeling captured by the question:
'What has become of our children?' In this chapter I want to
undertake a parallel enquiry, one that asks what kind of society we
have created, and which is summed up in the agonized question:
'What will become of our children?' This latter theme is a
common one in Christian discussions, where there are long
descriptions of the awful world in which children must grow to
maturity, and in which they prematurely lose their innocence. The
Church of England report *All God's Children*, for example,
asserts that: 'elements in our society are combining to create for
today's children a prematurely adult and somewhat lonely world
that accustoms them to materialism, hedonism, selfishness, sexual
amorality, the unseriousness and even normality of violence, the
possibility of spiritual power through an openness to the occult –
and all this against an ever-weakening acknowledgement of the

truth and relevance of Christianity.'[2] In fact, the idea of childhood as a time of innocence separated out from the adult world is a relatively recent Western idea. Up until the last few hundred years (as still in many cultures today), different views of childhood allowed children to share adult life and experience. Perhaps the anxiety to keep children innocent reflects our dissatisfaction with the kind of society we adults have built.

The volume of childhood distress across our land is vast. Some 98,000 children run away from home each year, and several thousand calls a day are made to the telephone help service Childline.[3] Child sexual abuse runs at high levels – and is a common reason why children run away or seek help. It is difficult to know whether more children than ever before are suffering, or whether it is only that reporting and recognition of abuse has increased. Children in the past suffered from a harsh physical environment, but today it seems they are more likely to suffer psychological distress. There are rising rates of teenage suicide, depression, anorexia, and increasing drug abuse. Family breakdown may be a contributory factor in some of these cases, but many of them reflect what is happening in society generally: distorted views of sexuality and power, attitudes towards the female body and food, competitiveness, hopelessness, the easy availability of drugs. In one survey of teenage views in 1993, though 70 per cent felt life was really worth living, 26 per cent had considered taking their own life.[4]

Poverty is a reality for many children, especially those in one-parent families. Poor housing and unemployment increase the pressures on families, and social class still affects what opportunities are available for young people. Racism makes its presence felt for many children from minority ethnic groups, both in the growing number of racially motivated attacks, and in the way they are disadvantaged in the education system and the jobs market. Girls throughout society still face discrimination because of their sex, and boys are pressurized by the expectations of masculinity. These factors, just as much as the negative values that *All God's Children* reports, make it very difficult to be a child growing up in the Britain of the 1990s.[5]

The impact of social policy

Though there has been much talk about the importance of 'The Family', it has had a limited effect on legislation. One exception is the 1989 Children Act, an important piece of legislation to which I shall return in later chapters. It makes children's interests paramount, and seeks to meet these within their families wherever possible. It has been important for children's welfare that their perspective and their rights as individuals have been recognized, but in several areas family life has been negatively affected by legislation. Immigration rules have been tightened up and serve to split up Black and Asian families. Child benefit has been frozen or under threat over the last decade, and looks likely to disappear in time. It is criticized as an anachronistic universal welfare benefit, though its origins are as a tax allowance which takes account of the extra responsibilities of families with children. Tax allowances to support the burden of buying a house, or buying a pension, or taking out private medical care are not denied to those who 'don't need them'. Yet support for the burden of rearing a family is regarded in this way, as if having children were rather like having a new car or an expensive holiday. Maternity rights for employed women have been cut back, and Britain has a particularly poor record amongst European Union members on such things as nursery and childcare provision and parental leave. This was brought home to me at a conference in 1993 when MEP Christine Crawley swiftly listed provision made for families across Europe. Under every heading bar one, the United Kingdom was near the bottom. The exception was our provision of housing for single mothers, though this may simply reflect that we have a greater number of single, homeless mothers in the first place.[6]

Politicians argue about the precise form of support which families ought to have, but there is a need for proper co-ordination of the way different departmental policies impact on families, as well as for additional, 'family-friendly' policies. A number of organizations have put together proposals of this nature, and it is to be hoped that these will get a hearing during the International Year of the Family in 1994. Organizations have their own agendas, but there is agreement about a number of measures which would support family life rather than undermine it.

However, it is not only policies that have an effect: the values on which they are based also leave their mark. Two elements have been central in the thinking of the Right over the last decade and a half: the individual's right to free choice, and the pre-eminence of the market. We live in a culture which promotes the individual rather than the corporate, and the Left as well as the Right has been influenced by this. The idea that individual rights are important has a long history, and can be traced back to the Enlightenment at least. But the way in which the values of individual enterprise and responsibility, autonomy and freedom of choice were promoted in the 1980s did mark a change. There was much less stress on the values of doing things in community. As Margaret Thatcher famously put it: 'There is no such thing as society. There are in-dividuals and there are families.' Instead of dependence on the state, people have been urged to stand on their own feet, and to buy private pensions or health care. Rather than having to join a trade union closed shop, individual workers are able to opt out – the individual right to choose takes precedence over the possible interests of workers as a group. Instead of high taxes corporately funding costly public services, people are to choose how they spend their income – giving to charity if they want to support others, not doing it through taxation.[7]

The rights of consumers were increasingly promoted, and the Citizens' Charter idea reflected this. Yet an over-emphasis on consumer rights can be damaging. Doctors may be over-cautious for fear of being sued if things go wrong – for example, the number of Caesarian births goes up. Large compensation claims may harm an organization which already faces funding difficulties – which is why I felt a little guilty when I got compensation for delayed journeys from British Rail (pre-privatization)! That we simply cannot have the kind of society we want if we concentrate exclusively on individual rights, is not always recognized. There was a telling example of this in an article by John Major, where he insisted that people want 'to be independent; they want to choose schools, holidays, where they live, how they live. They don't want others telling them what to do. They want better prospects for their children. . . . They want security in their old age and they want a more courteous and a safer society; one in which the law is respected and crime is punished.'[8] The fundamental contradiction here is that law and order relies on people doing what they are told. The hidden assumption is that society is divided between decent people who are free to make their good choices, and an underclass who commit crime and need to learn to do as they are told.

The individual is seen as a free agent in a competitive market economy, but the market, by its very nature, has little room for co-operation, altruism, and accepting responsibility for others. Though many companies try to put something back into the community, understandably their eyes are still firmly on what is in it for them. Some people have suggested to me that schools and companies are much less likely to have a corporate ethic and sense of identity than in the past. Though I am not sure about this, it is possible to detect a trend away from companies or organizations keeping a strong identity for their workforce, towards contracting out work to small units or freelance operators. There is an ideological bias against large public corporations – though not against private multinational companies. Nationalization had its problems, and reform of service industries, the railways, and so on was clearly needed. Yet in selling off nationalized industries, we also seem to have sold off part of our sense of being a nation, of owning things in common. The times when the interests of the nation have been most clearly asserted have been over against the European Union, where even supporters of closer ties were insisting that what we wanted as an individual nation was more important than compromising and acting for the sake of a larger whole. This has interesting parallels with the Church of England's proceedings over women priests, which placed a much higher premium on individual conscience than on community decision-making. In few walks of life do we expect, or are we expected, to put aside our desires and convictions for the sake of the group. Fragmentation is both the political and spiritual order of the day.

Individualism

Selfish individualism has been highlighted by many Christians as the godless spirit of the age. Moynagh, for example, speaks of the 'self-please ethic' which dominates society, and leads to marriage break-up and inadequate parenting.[9] Clifford Longley, writing in *The Daily Telegraph*, blames the crisis in the family on the modern emphasis on the pursuit of human happiness. He calls for religious leaders to challenge this by saying that 'the route to happiness is by way of renunciation: happiness through unselfish love.' Family life must not be designed around the right of parents to pursue their own happiness.[10] It is true that where ideas about individual rights and the encouragement of individual fulfilment are current, without a parallel emphasis on caring for one another and valuing community, a society is likely to run into trouble. Yet individualism also has a very positive side. Whether or not we agree with the political solutions which have been tried in the name of free choice and individual rights, most of us would find it very difficult to be given no say as individuals in our personal lives. There is a strong strand in Christian tradition which gives the individual conscience before God a high priority, even where this means going against government, family, or even the church authorities.

Theologians today readily speak about sacrificial service, caring concern, and social responsibility towards society's victims, and in discourse about the family it is predominantly women who are the focus. Because it is women who have responsibility for 'keeping the family together', it is their supposed selfishness which is blamed for causing the problems, and their self-sacrifice which can bring about a solution. Such commentators argue that women ought to stay in unsatisfactory marriages, or refrain from full-time employment, to care for family members – whatever the cost to themselves. I have already explored these issues at length in *A Woman's Work*,[11] and pointed out how these assumptions can prevent women from being all they are and should be. It is important for women to be seen as individuals who matter in their own right, yet this can go alongside valuing the well-being of others. Service of others and self-fulfilment are interconnected values, not mutually exclusive. David Sinclair, addressing a conference on 'Dependency in Culture and Society', suggests that we ought to talk about personhood rather than individuality, for the former holds us together in relationships, whilst the latter sets us apart. The Church must affirm that personal, relational existence is the 'road along which the journey of redemption must pass'.[12] This is a common theme in Christian writing, and it has been developed by feminist theologians like Mary Grey, who emphasizes the importance of 'mutuality in relating'.[13] It is not that people should strive to be autonomous and independent of all others, but that they should be able to be themselves in relationship with others around them.

Because the crisis in family life has been so quickly defined as a result of too much individualism, few commentators seem to acknowledge the positive side it has, especially for women. Michael Ignatieff, writing in the *Observer*, is one of the few who does. It should be obvious, he believes, that single motherhood would decline if girls learnt enough at school to value themselves, and had the prospect of jobs. The girls on welfare 'get pregnant, not because they want so much but because they accept so little. A dose of hedonist individualism – wanting more out of your life than teenage motherhood – might give them the motivation to delay child-rearing until they were ready for it.' Ignatieff recognizes, too, the struggle which both women and men are going through to try to balance the needs of parents and children in a satisfactory way: 'You can tell a gloomy story about noble family values being eroded by the hedonistic individualism of our age. Or you can tell a much less pessimistic story about families engaged in an evolving search to reconcile the needs of children with the legitimate aspirations of parents', he says. 'It's not a simple conflict between selfishness and duty, but between conflicting roles and between family values and parents' aspirations, both good in themselves, but often irreconcilable.'[14] The question we need to go on to ask is why the needs of parents and children are so often in conflict, and whether there are any other ways of organizing society that could reduce this tension. We need to work for a balance between individual responsibility and our wider public obligations, between commitment to family and relationships, and to our own personal development.

Employment and family life

The debate about how this might be done has not been central to the political agenda. The idea that as much as possible should be left to the market dominated political decision-making through the 1980s and early 1990s. Around it clustered other elements: the need to be cost-effective, the value of competition, the principle of non-intervention, the removal of restrictions and 'red tape', and the high value placed on material things, money, and goods. Perhaps some form of market economy is the only effective model for successful industrialized nations, but there is still room for intervention, and a society which is deeply concerned about family life will look at the ways in which this cluster of ideas affects families and social life. Of particular importance was the idea that families were considered largely to be private affairs, and that it was the market which would decide the relationship between family and employment. Thus it was up to employers to provide childcare facilities if, as happened briefly in the mid-1980s, they needed to woo mothers into employment. The prime motivation was not what was best for children or mothers, but the profitability of the business.

There is a lack of any strategic approach to the problem of fitting employment with family life, and this can cause great stress in families. Yet most workers try to keep their domestic lives separate from their employment, at whatever cost to themselves and their families. Society too bears that cost – through the strains on parent-child relationships, on marriages, and through having to fund welfare benefits where a parent cannot afford to work because of the expense of childcare, or the absence of alternative care for other dependants. Though there are employers who make provision for parents or carers, and there are organizations which provide nurseries and out-of-school care, childcare provision in Britain is very piecemeal. It is often a matter of cobbling together precarious arrangements, which collapse all too easily when a child is ill, or a school rearranges a training day. Most parents, and mothers in particular, find it hard to fit satisfactory employment and family life together. If the needs of small children are for stability of care, many may not be getting the best deal.

Still behind much discussion of families and the workplace lies the assumption that mothers ought not to be in employment, at least whilst children are small. Delinquency is sometimes blamed on the increased numbers of mothers in employment, although studies show no significant connection between the two.[15] Nor is there evidence that being in day-care of itself damages children.

30

Whether it proves problematic or not will depend on how good the day-care is: whether it provides loving, consistent care directed towards the child's developmental needs. It will also depend on how well the relationship is built up with the mother and/or father at other times, and what the situation would have been if the mother herself had looked after the child full time.

We have to recognize that the practice in this country of isolating mothers with their young children is a fairly recent and narrow way of doing things. It has contributed to a number of problems in families, with a high incidence of depression among mothers, abuse of children, and over-intense relationships with offspring. A more usual and more balanced way is for mothers and children to be part of a community, sharing childcare and the socialization of children. This pattern still exists strongly in some working-class areas, and among minority ethnic groups, and happens in an informal way in many other communities. West Indian mothers speak of shared care as positively good for a child. Asian mothers are less likely to be working outside the home, but rely on the support of their community in the work of raising children – and may experience difficulties if they find themselves isolated away from it.[16] The answer is not simply to demand that the government spend more, but it is surely wrong to leave it entirely to the market to decide how parents are treated in the labour force, and what provision is made for children. If we are serious in our concern for families, we need to acknowledge that fitting family life with employment is our corporate responsibility.

The future for young people

Another area where serious questions need to be raised is in the treatment of young people. Much is being done with the education system in Britain, with some much needed reforms, and the intro-duction of a National Curriculum. There has been an emphasis on getting pupils to think for themselves, and not just to absorb information to regurgitate for exams – though some still push for a return to 'old-style' learning. Schools are much more likely to encourage both children and parents to participate in decisions about school life and behaviour policy; local management of schools and parental choice have been key concepts. Many schools do make these reforms work well, but too little attention has been given to the needs of schools and pupils who find it difficult to be self-motivating. Competition between schools has contributed to an increase in the number of exclusions of difficult pupils, and local authorities are now less likely to be able to afford to do the intensive work with them which might achieve results. Yet surely it is essential that attention is given to children with behaviour problems, if they are not going to develop into the antisocial toughs who create such fear in their communities. There are a number of approaches that do seem to work with such children, but they are costly, and can attract few resources in a competitive educational system. The Burger King chain has stepped into this gap by sponsoring a college for school drop-outs, though whether it should be left to private enterprise to pick up a few pieces here and there, rather than having a central strategy, is a major question. Many people are concerned about the way retailers now offer school equipment in exchange for parents' spending in their stores.

It is of the utmost importance for a society to allow its children to grow into responsible adulthood, as I noted in the previous chapter. Yet through much of the last two decades, young people have had no automatic path to follow into employment, and some seem to have no realistic prospect of ever having a job. It is no longer even true that children who work hard and do well at school, or even go on to get degrees, will get good jobs. Young people can be forgiven for thinking there is more money and credibility to be made in being entrepreneurial on the street, stealing cars for example, than in trying to be a good citizen. Those without special skills are wanted less and less as automation and rationalization continue through industries. The 1989 Employment Act removed restrictions on terms and conditions of work for young people, on the grounds that the ability to use cheap labour is what makes Britain competitive.[17] This may be the case, and clearly the government sees this as benefiting the economy as a whole. In theory, it ought to mean that it is easier for young people to get jobs, but the fact that they are not protected by having a statutory minimum wage has led to their exploitation (and has undercut other workers). Children as young as age ten have been found doing factory shifts, and young teenagers have been killed or injured at work, where proper safety procedures have not been implemented. Rather than being launched into steady employment, teenagers may lose their jobs once they become old enough to need paying more.[18]

Some would say that if all protective legislation were lifted, there would be many more jobs, and the country would become more prosperous. It is ethically extremely questionable whether we ought to go far down this line: labourers are worthy of their hire, and people's labour ought not to be exploited through minimal wages, the absence of safety standards, or the absence of any employees' rights. Also, in the context of this book, we need to ask what value is placed on people when their labour is treated in this way? What message is given to young people, or to older people who are made redundant, or who are unemployed for years on end? I heard a commentator say recently that today's young people are the first generation who can expect a lower standard of living than their parents had; if this is true, the question 'What will become of our children?' is even more pertinent.

We are, it has been said, a society which knows the cost of everything and the value of nothing. I don't think this is entirely true, but the statement reflects something about where we are. The market has been introduced into many areas formerly regarded as being of public service. Hospitals, schools, social services, even parts of the Church, have been required to make profit and efficiency their core values. Efficiency is important, and of course organizations should be accountable for how they spend their funds; but we cannot make these values pre-eminent, and then complain if people are not prepared to give something for nothing. As Robin Gill points out, a strategy which speaks purely about being functional and efficient is ignoring values which are essential to doing the job. Many people go into the health care services, or education with a sense of vocation, because they care. Care requires pragmatism and moral passion, says Gill. Without pragmatism, it becomes dissipated and ineffective. Without moral passion, it loses its very heart.[19] There is immense frustration evident amongst workers in these areas, who feel that their desire to care is being thrown back in their faces. Such frustration easily leads to people becoming cynical and falling back on their rights, whereas before they had often gone 'the extra mile'.

A material world

It is common to blame present-day ills on the materialistic, individualistic culture we now have. It is true that the sheer volume of easily stealable consumer goods is one factor in the rise in crime. Indeed, changes in the crime rate correlate with trends in economic consumption to some extent. Yet materialism has been a feature of life for much of this century – the 1930s crime wave was blamed on the 'acquisitive consumer society' of that decade, for example. One thing that has changed significantly is technology, and in particular communication and information systems. Advertising is an integral part of this, and the speedy way in which we produce, hype, and disseminate information these days has its effect on the values we live by. It is especially significant that children are targeted as an important consumer group, with whole ranges of products being marketed on the strength of one character, film, or television programme. Children have gone through crazes for generations, with all the pressure that that puts on parents, but it is possible to exploit this so much more efficiently in today's society.

There is a lot of Christian concern with what children watch on television, a concern that has arisen particularly in the United States, where children watch a great deal of unregulated broadcasting. In fact, British television still provides a lot of creative programming, and television can be an entertaining and informative medium if watched with discrimination. Unlimited viewing by children is not likely to be healthy, even if it does not cause personality problems or antisocial behaviour in any simple, straightforward way. Martin Herbert offers some sensible comments on this, reminding us that adults have always made a scapegoat of the latest newcomer to the mass media – novels, films, radio, comics – for their failure to produce perfect children. Yet, he says, next to 'the influences which we definitely *know* to predispose children to hostile behaviour – hostile, rejecting and punitive parents, and (in the case of teenagers) excessive alcohol, violent peers and so on – the . . . entertainments of childhood seem to pale into insignificance'.[20] However, I am more worried by children's access to pornographic and/or violent videos and computer games, and wonder what the cumulative effect is of being saturated with those values at the expense of more caring and less exploitative ones?

Ann Wilson Schaef is scathing about the value system which she categorizes as the 'Addictive System'. Though she speaks of American culture, what she says has echoes for Britain too: 'Pride, covetousness, lust, anger, gluttony, envy, and sloth – the sins that are traditionally deemed fatal to spiritual progress – are woven . . . into the very fabric of the Addictive System', she writes. 'We live in a system that exploits the bodies of women, children, and men to sell products. We live in a system that sets up increasingly elaborate and complex agencies to control and regulate dishonesty – agencies that time and again prove dishonest themselves.'[21]   Brake and Hale discuss similar issues in *Public Order and Private Lives*, which looks critically at what has happened in Britain over the last fourteen years. They find on the one hand, 'distinct signs of social discontent, with its disorder, violence and increase in crime, and on the other hand, the cynical self-advancement of the enterprise culture which prioritises individuality over social responsibility'. They comment on corporate crime and tax evasion, and the collective abdications of responsibility when disasters such as the sinking of the *Herald of Free Enterprise* and the *Marchioness* occurred. 'A moral climate has been created in which collective responsibility has become unfashionable', they say.

Integrity in public life seems to be a rare commodity. We hear of few cases where politicians and business people 'do the honourable thing' and resign when found guilty of mismanagement. Far more seem to try to cling on to their jobs as long as possible, or negotiate an excessive 'golden handshake'. Confronted with issues like growing homelessness, poverty, or unemployment, most politicians quote figures which prove there isn't a problem, or blame the individuals concerned, rather than showing real concern. At the general election in April 1992, what struck me most was the lack of integrity amongst politicians of all sides. The whole thing seemed to be a carefully orchestrated advertising campaign from different brand leaders. It was all about projecting the right image, and using the right words and pictures, rather than addressing issues and admitting it might be tough solving them. Even politicians I had formerly respected for their integrity seemed to be willing to say anything in pursuit of re-election. Some months after the election, we learned that the promise made by the Conservatives that they (unlike Labour) would not put up taxes, had a very short shelf-life. Promises were statements of what was believed at the time, not commitments for the future, we were told.

With this kind of thinking at the heart of government, and shared by politicians on all sides, how can values of commitment, loyalty, trust, and integrity be encouraged in the nation as a whole? As children, we absorbed what our parents did rather than what they said, and as citizens we are more influenced by what politicians do than by what they tell us we should think. One of the values Christians are called to uphold is integrity, being honest, principled, trustworthy, and consistent. Living with integrity is risky. We·are just as likely to end up getting crucified as finding that people respect us for being honest about what we believe. Yet we need more people prepared to demonstrate this quality if there is to be any positive change in values in society as a whole.

Notes

1. W. H. Auden, 'The Shield of Achilles', in E. Mendelson, ed., Collected Poems (London, Faber & Faber).

2. *All God's Children* (London, National Society/Church House Publishing, 1991), pp. 32-3.

3. M. Phillips, ed., *The Parent Trap* (Guardian Studies, vol. 4, 1991), p. 5.

4. Quoted on a television programme in May 1993.

5. For a fuller discussion of these sociological factors, see N. Abercrombie et al., *Contemporary British Society* (Cambridge, Polity Press, 1988).

6. Women's National Commission conference on 'The Family in Europe', March 1993.

7. In fact, the rise in indirect taxes offset cuts in income tax for many wage earners, but this was the philosophy which was put forward.

8. *Oxford Mail*, 8 September 1993.

9. M. Moynagh, *Home to Home* (London, Daybreak, 1990).

10. C. Longley, writing in *The Daily Telegraph*, 12 March 1993.

11. A. Borrowdale, *A Woman's Work* (London, SPCK, 1989).

12. D. Sinclair, *Dependency* (University of Edinburgh, Centre for Theology and Public Issues, 1988), p. 10.

13. M. Grey, *Redeeming the Dream* (London, SPCK, 1989).

14. M. Ignatieff, *Observer*, 7 March 1993.

15. See D. Utting, J. Bright, and C. Henricson, *Crime and the Family* (London, Family Policy Studies Centre, 1993).

16. Experiences of motherhood in different ethnic groups are described in A. Wilson, *Finding a Voice* (London, Virago, 1978); K. Stone, 'Motherhood and waged work', in A. Phizacklea, ed., *One Way Ticket* (London, Routledge & Kegan Paul, 1983); and Y. Alibhai, in K. Gieve, ed., *Balancing Acts* (London, Virago, 1989).

17. Although this conflicts with European Union directives.

18. *Observer*, 15 November 1992.

19. R. Gill, *Moral Communities* (Exeter, University of Exeter Press, 1992).

20. M. Herbert, *Discipline* (Oxford, Basil Blackwell, 1989), p. 130. David Porter gives some useful tips for parents in *Children at Risk* (Eastbourne, Kingsway, 1986), offering a sensible approach to television, films, computer games, and so on. It is interesting how dated some of the book sounds, though it was only published in 1986.

21. A. Schaef, *When Society Becomes an Addict* (San Francisco, Harper & Row, 1988), pp. 132-3.

chapter three

Whose Family?
What Crisis?

*All through the scriptures we find the husband and wife
and their children as a unique social unit. . . . God has
set the nuclear family apart as a distinct unit.*

S. Grunlan[1]

*We have dealt with the family as household. The future
lies in dealing with family as a set of relationships.*

W. Clark[2]

*All feminist and pseudo-libertarian raving on the issue
should be treated with contempt. The family may be the
source of many woes, but it is also the only source of our
happiness and stability. Neither is there any serious
division on the view that the conventional family is
seriously threatened and that this is a threat to the whole
of society.*

B. Appleby[3]

Amidst troubled times and changing values, most families muddle
along. The rhetoric about 'The Family' and moral decline apply to
other people's failures and never our own, for talk about 'The
Family' and experience of family life, often seem worlds apart.
Part of the reason for this is that the word 'family' has a number
of distinct meanings. The *Collins Dictionary* definition includes
four quite different understandings: 'family' can mean parents and
offspring, one's children as distinguished from one's spouse, a
group descended from a common ancestor, or all the persons

living together in one household. I would add to that the notion of 'The Family' (with capital letters) as a sacred institution which, though it relates to the other meanings, has its own ideological and theological significance. These different definitions suggest that there are three basic ways in which we talk about the family. I should like to examine these in more depth, because the idea that the family is in crisis does not apply equally to all of them.

Kith and kin

Firstly, we use the word to describe the set of people we are related to by bonds of blood or affection – our 'kith and kin', in the old phrase. My family are the people I'm connected to, and I may use the word either for my family of origin, or my husband and children, or sometimes for the wider network of family which includes all my children's relations. That very general understanding of family as 'the people I'm connected to' can easily include a son's live-in girlfriend, or the friend an aunt has lived with for thirty years – whether there's a sexual relationship there or not. 'Family' can also extend to unrelated people who have been important, such as a godmother, or neighbour – or even pets. A 'family party' might well include such people, where the emphasis is on belonging to a close network rather than on a legal or ideological definition of what a family is. Sue Walrond-Skinner offers the definition of family as 'an intimate domestic group, in which individuals are committed to one another by ties of blood, law, habitation or emotional bonds, or a combination of all four'.[4] Blood ties often do have a special significance: we may dislike our relatives, have nothing to do with them, yet still be aware of being connected to them. However, neither they nor legal ties determine exactly who is regarded as family.

Family in this sense is not dead. Family groups of one sort or another are much in evidence around us – enjoying themselves, shopping, consuming, arguing, doing things together. When most of us talk about 'my family', we are referring either to our immediate relations, or that wider group; and it is important that we affirm the family in this sense. We can do with being encouraged to care for those who are connected to us, to think of 'family' as an open system which looks outside the nuclear family. This wider view of family is at the heart of Peter Pothan's helpful booklet *Unpackaging the Family*. He takes Western theologians to task for their narrow assumptions about family form. He points out that they have swallowed the idea of the nuclear family structure as the universal building-block of society, and interpreted biblical teaching as if it were about the same thing. Yet 'the original family structure in most ancient societies was in fact the residential extended family', and it is this rather than the nuclear family which is found not only in the Old Testament, but also among Jews, Greeks, and Romans in New Testament times. The Genesis description of a man leaving his parents and cleaving to his wife refers to sexual love between man and woman, and is not a statement about family form, since a couple would not live in isolation from other family members.[5]

Similarly, we have to regard the idea that the nuclear family has always been the norm in British or European history with some caution. Though grandparents were not common when life expectancy was shorter, households might well contain unmarried brothers or sisters as well as servants or apprentices. There is disagreement about when the nuclear family first appeared, and how widespread it was, but it does seem to have arrived later rather than earlier in European history. Pothan suggests it reached Europe in the Middle Ages, and grew with urbanization and industrialization. Changes in family form are allied to the changing demands of the economy – and this is equally true of the particular patterns we have today. Historically there has always been a variety of family types, and individual families changed their form over time, as they do today.[6]

The extended family in both residential and non-residential forms does seem to have had a significant place in the past, and continues today. The residential extended family still exists where people take in elderly parents, and even where people are not living near one another, they keep their links through regular visits and telephone calls in a way that was not possible in previous eras. What we think of as nuclear families are not isolated, but part of a network of relationships with kin and others. Many families in Britain actually see themselves as a 'non-residential extended family', rather in the way I have described. An elderly relative living alone or a young adult working away –

or indeed, children with families of their own – are part of the family structure, not alienated from it. Women in particular value family networks – I probably know more about the grandchildren, siblings, and parents of my women friends and work colleagues than I do about the nuclear families of my male friends and colleagues. Perhaps we have ended up with narrow definitions of the family because they have been drawn up by men who have not been so aware of the importance of family networks (they have only seen the phone bill), but I'm not sure this stands up to analysis!

This rather open-ended understanding of family seems to fit more accurately with people's real experience. It is interesting that the 1988 Lambeth Conference refused to put boundaries around the definition of 'family' when it asserted: 'We believe that the family, whether a unit of one parent and children, an adult child and an elderly parent, adult relatives, a husband, wife and children, or *whatever other shape*, is the fundamental institution of human community.'[7] For many in the churches insist that people need a norm set out to follow. They want the Church to affirm a particular form of family, and though they talk about being caring for those outside the correct forms, it is in fact very hard to do both. It is interesting that Jesus himself widened the definition of 'family' to mean those who do God's will: it is *they* who are his brothers and sisters and mother. Yet it is in Jesus' name that many want to limit the family to only one form. (I shall look again at the question of norms or absolutes in Chapter 11.) But Anderson needs heeding when he states that the pastoral theologian's agenda is 'not to identify a "Christian family" but to help people find ways of being Christian in families'.[8]

The household

Secondly, 'the family' can be defined in fairly specific sociological terms. This is necessary to get accurate statistics about households, and in order to apply social policy. The most usual idea is that a family consists of a couple, or perhaps a single parent, and their children, and ceases to exist when the children leave and set up their own families. Thus the General Household Survey uses the word to describe married or cohabiting couples on their own or with children, or lone parents and children. Children here means children who are part of the parents' household, have never themselves been married, and have no children of their own. A single mother who moves in with her parents creates a two-family household. The key element here is the presence of dependent children – and this is the definition of family for all sorts of leisure facilities. I cannot travel cheaply on my Family Railcard with my husband, mother, or sister unless we take a child under sixteen with us – though the child does not have to be related.

The family as household is facing change, and the statistics reflecting this change contribute to the fear that the family is in crisis. There are big demographic changes which are having a profound effect on society: the proportion of elderly people is growing steadily, and contrasts with the predominantly young society that existed in previous eras. Some 200 years ago, half the population of Western Europe was under twenty, but now only a quarter of it is.[9] But the real concern in Britain is preserved for changing sexual morality, and the trend away from combining sex and childrearing in one life-long monogamous relationship towards more variety in family form. This is not so much a falling away from what has always been the case as a return to some of the variety which existed before. However, because of the stage we are at, we cannot yet tell whether we are on the road to disaster, or moving towards something that will in the end be more conducive to the health of individuals and society. The worry for many people is that by the time we can tell accurately, it will be too late to do anything.

The situation can seem stark. Since 1971, marriages have fallen by a fifth, whilst divorces have doubled. It seems likely that a quarter of all children will experience the divorce of their parents before they reach the age of sixteen. If current trends continue, by the year 2000, only half of all British children will live with natural parents who were married when they were born and who stay married until they are grown up. There is a large increase in cohabitation, the illegitimacy ratio is increasing, and there is a growing number of one-parent families. These trends are not spread evenly throughout the country, however. For example, a higher percentage of adults cohabit in the south of Britain (excluding London) than in the north.[10] Areas like the south

43

coast have a high proportion of one- and two-person households, while inner cities have a higher proportion of multi-adult households. Bangladeshi and Pakistani families are more likely to fall into the 'traditional' nuclear family pattern than white families: two-thirds of households in their communities consist of husband, wife, and dependent children, as compared to less than a quarter of the white population, and over a half of Indian households. West Indian families often show a different pattern, with more common-law marriage, and households with a mother or grand-mother at the head.[11]

The increasing number of women who have children outside marriage is a trend that causes widespread concern. In 1991, 30 per cent of live births were outside marriage. This figure was very low (1%) for the Pakistani/Bangladeshi community, and high (48%) for mothers born in the Caribbean, reflecting different social patterns. The trend reflects the situation in some other parts of Europe – a half of all births are outside marriage in Sweden, Denmark, and France. However, three-quarters of births outside marriage are registered by both parents, and a half by parents living at the same address. Though they represent a minority of such births, it is single, unsupported mothers who attract the most attention. As I noted in Chapter 2, they are castigated as a new underclass who deliberately sponge off the state, but it is worth remembering that illegitimacy is an age-old phenomenon. For example, one estimate is that a third of brides were pregnant in the early eighteenth and nineteenth centuries.[12] And the severe moral censure of births outside marriage, which some would like to see reintroduced, left a grim trail in its wake. Both children and mothers suffered, as is reflected in novels like George Eliot's *Adam Bede*, or Dickens's *Bleak House*. Even if the system which we now have for supporting single mothers is far from perfect, it is surely an improvement on the harsh treatment meted out to them in the past.

Alongside the notion of the family in decline, we do need to set the advances that have been made over the last century. A BBC 2 series early in 1993, *A Labour of Love*, traced the experiences of families between the wars. Recollections of that era tend to be nostalgic about how good times were: 'we were poor, but we were happy'. Yet here were elderly people speaking of the harsh realities of bringing up children when infant mortality was high, poverty and unhealthy living conditions were a feature of many people's lives, and the Second World War took a heavy physical and emotional toll on all family members. It was a reminder of why the Welfare State, currently being dismantled by slow degrees, was thought necessary. It also indicated just how harsh life was for women. Indeed, women's changed expectations have been one of the most influential factors affecting families this century, and many external factors have changed things for women. There has been a large increase of mothers in the labour market, and women are more equal in law. Reliable contraception has made an incredible difference to women's lives, as has better health and a dramatic lowering of the risks of dying in childbirth. Men have been much more slow to adjust and, as I shall argue in Chapter 5, the differences in women's and men's expectations of marriage and relationships is one reason for the high rate of divorce and cohabitation we now have.

The Family

Thirdly, there is 'The Family', the institution which is variously said to be the bedrock of society, or the God-given unit for building society. It is usually modelled on the patriarchal nuclear family: father as breadwinner and head of the house, mother either not employed or working in a secondary job, and dependent children. Alternative forms may be tolerated by some, but for others they just don't count. O. R. Johnston, in his book *Who Needs the Family?*, suggests that most people 'have an in-built reluctance to accord the word "family" to the tragic figure of an unsupported mother and her children'.[13] For him, it is the nuclear family, with a man at its head, which is the only proper family, and the one ordained by God. The unsupported mother is a tragic figure in need of help, who cannot hold together life as a family. This is hardly a view which supports lone parents in the difficult task they have of providing a stable home life for their children.

There have indeed been times when the nuclear family defined in this way was the norm. One of the classic sociological definitions, Murdock's 1949 statement, proclaimed that this was what the family was: 'a social group characterised by common residence, economic co-operation and reproduction. It includes adults of both sexes, at least two of whom maintain a socially approved sexual relationship, and one or more children, own or adopted, of the sexually co-habiting adults.'[14] However, this could never be a universal truth. Different cultures can have very different ways of arranging marriage, procreation and sex which do not always involve men and women living together. As Edholm says: 'The family, particularly the nuclear family, can be seen, through comparative analysis, as just one very specific means of organizing the relationships between parents and children, males and females . It is not, as has often been claimed, some kind of "natural", instinctive and "sacred" unit.'[15]

Murdock pointed out that most societies have needs related to reproduction, sexuality, socialization of children, and maintenance (i.e. economic support, residence, and protection), and that they use family structures to meet these requirements. This is true, but the family structures created do not have the standard form he assumed. *Kibbutzim* are well-known examples of a different way of raising children; and in some matrilineal societies men do not live with their permanent wives, and only visit women for sexual purposes. Women may have sexual relationships with any number of men, and not know who their children's father is. The world-wide Church has not always found it easy to come to terms with cultural diversity in marriage and family life. Polygamy has been a perennial problem for the Church in Africa, for example. A meeting of the Anglican Consultative Council and Anglican Primates, discussing cohabitation in 1993 in Cape Town, seemed more prepared to distinguish between casual relationships and more ordered ones, or 'faithful concupiscence', as it was termed. Even if monogamous pairing for the purposes of having children is the most common way of organizing family life, this will still cover a number of variations.[16] Expectations about men's role in marriage and childrearing vary considerably, and living arrangements take many different forms – with geography and economic status being key determining factors.

Family, Bible, and theology

Unfortunately, Christian writers who want to uphold the patriarchal nuclear family form as God-given, ignore the sociological and anthropological evidence of different ways of organizing family. They may even read back the nuclear family into the Bible, and claim it is biblical and therefore divine – Grunlan's view quoted at the start of this chapter is just one example of this. Ortlund gives the clarion call to Christians: 'Don't try to shape your family to some former day. *Don't go back to yesterday; go back to the Bible instead.*'[17] The mind boggles at this: are Christian husbands to sleep with the daily help if their wives can't have children (Gen. 16.1-4) or have two wives (Gen. 29.21-30)? Much of what is advised is a reading back into the Bible of values and methods specific to the writer's culture. Even if the call is not to follow specific examples, but instead the general pattern, it is hard to understand, since – as Pothan has pointed out – the most common family form during the biblical era is the residential extended family and not the nuclear family which Ortlund describes. Interestingly, the word 'family' is used comparatively rarely in the Old Testament, and only once in the New – where the reference is to 'every family in earth and heaven'. The Old Testament speaks largely of 'families', in the sense of clans, rather than about what we would recognize as a nuclear family, and paints a picture of destructive relationships as well as revealing God at work.

As with most other issues, seeking guidance from the Bible about how to organize family life today is not a simple process. The Bible is a very complex work, consisting of many different books written over many centuries, and reflecting a lot of different ideas about women, men, society, and even the nature of God. If we are to use the Bible for guidance, we need to look for the principles underlying the text, and see how those apply today, rather than assume every verse demands our obedience. For Barton, the fact that the Bible is full of descriptions of laws and customs points 'to God's care for people in their common [including sexual and domestic] life and to the importance of love of neighbour in response'.[18] As John Rogerson points out, the New Testament injunction that wives be subject to husbands reflects beliefs of that day, and is an attempt to interpret contemporary marriage in the light of the gospel. Today's Christians, therefore, 'can best appropriate [this] by realising that they are to attempt to do something similar in their own setting – to bring to bear what they hold to be the heart of the Christian message, on the marriage conventions of their time.' Rogerson concludes: 'The Bible is not there to provide us with laws, it is there to guide communities of faith.' The New Testament shows us 'a new community wrestling with every day problems in the light of the *new dynamic* brought by Jesus Christ', and this is the task for contemporary Christians as well.[19]

We cannot therefore simply lift phrases from the Bible such as '"I hate divorce" says the Lord God of Israel' (Mal. 2.16), as Ortlund does, to show that divorce is wrong for couples today. The immediate context of the verse is God's hatred for the man who breaks his promise to be faithful to his wife. The wider context is a very different cultural understanding of marriage and women's position in society. There are also instances where God hates religious festivals (Amos 5.21) or usury (lending money at interest), which even fundamentalists rarely apply. We have to go through a process of interpretation before we can say *what* is relevant, and precisely *how* it should apply to us today. There are also many issues facing us which simply weren't around in biblical days: the possibility of test-tube babies, the freedom for women to choose between having children, having none, and paid employment.

There is a huge amount of popular material written for Christians about family, mostly from an evangelical standpoint, yet unfortunately much of it relies on too simplistic an approach to the Bible, and takes far too little account of sociological insights. Anderson and Guernsey, theologians who themselves write from an evangelical perspective, are deeply critical of such literature. They point out that unless the psychological knowledge of family relationships which the books often use is linked in with other perspectives, the end result is rather superficial.[20] Nor do those writers take much account of the psychological damage that can be caused by the claustrophobic nature of the modern nuclear family. This family form was common in the 1950s, for example, yet – as Friedan showed in *The Feminine Mystique*[21] – it put great pressures on both mothers and children. A social theology of the family has to recognize the ways in which school, employment, and culture as a whole interconnect with family life. Walrond-Skinner gives a useful summary of approaches to the family in different disciplines in *The Fulcrum and the Fire*, and shows how each contributes something to our understanding.

The theology of family which has developed in evangelical Protestantism has usually put the hierarchically ordered traditional family at its centre. Karl Barth makes much of the proper ordering of family relationships, for example.[22] Theologians may stress the covenant between husband and wife, which reflects that between God and humanity. Catholic theology takes a sacramental view of marriage, whereby God's grace is poured into families through a couple's mutual love and caring. Jack Dominian's writings draw on this tradition, although he moves on from it.[23] In both traditional Catholic and Protestant views, 'The Family' is seen as a divinely ordained symbol of social stability and moral virtue. This has made it difficult for the Church to look more critically at what actually happens within families, and has left it sounding defensive about the past rather than creative about the future.

This traditionalist view parallels some secular opinion. Appleby's comments, quoted at the beginning of this chapter, may be expressed less politely than those of many religious leaders, but the feeling is essentially the same. The liberal and feminist critique of 'The Family' is dismissed – yet both have much to offer. Liberal Protestantism, as Barton notes, sees 'The Family' as 'a focus for the development of human individuality, religious sensibility and mature personhood', and places a strong emphasis on the rights of the individual, especially the child. Barton also mentions liberation theology, with its focus on the need for solidarity with oppressed groups, including impoverished families. Feminist theologies may mirror this affirmation of family solidarity, or be critical of 'The Family' as a source of oppression for women. Barton suggests that 'like the biblical material in all its diversity and (sometimes) strangeness, these various and (sometimes) strange theological traditions constitute a resource of great value which represent the attempts of Christian communities in times past and present to develop a more godly social order'.[24] Barton's own view is that ' "the family" per se is not God-given', but it can be both a 'relationship and an institution where God's grace is experienced and where people can find nurture and healing' when it has not become demonic or perverted by sin.

The Bible and Christian tradition also provide a corrective to any idealization of the nuclear family, with elements that are actually quite anti-family. Jesus calls his disciples away from their homes for long periods, and says that unless someone hates their husband or wife, brother or sister, son or daughter, they cannot be his disciples. Paul thinks it preferable to remain unmarried, though grudgingly allows that it is better to marry than to burn. Many feminist theologians have been quick to pick up this aspect of biblical thought. O. R. Johnston seems to have temporarily forgotten these elements of biblical teaching when he states that 'Promises of "liberation" from family obligations come from the father of lies himself.'[25] The thrust of these 'anti-family' sayings is not so much that discipleship is only possible outside family relationships, but that the individual's calling to follow Christ must come first. The warning in our own day must be against idolizing 'The Family', and expecting that women in particular must inevitably be called to devote themselves wholly to family life.

Rosemary Ruether, in a series of articles in *New Blackfriars,* describes how, in the New Testament, 'the Christian community is seen as a new kind of family, a voluntary community gathered by personal faith, which stands in tension with the natural family or kinship group'.[26] The family that existed in New Testament times was not just a social unit, but a religious one, and it was tied to the state and public order. To depart from one's family religion was also to go against the nation. Hence Christianity was inherently subversive both of family and state. It was largely women and slaves who transmitted Christianity in the first four centuries, because it was much more serious for a male head of household to convert, since he would be seen as going against both the ancestral religion and the state. Ruether sees the New Testament household codes as exploring the tensions in divided households, where a woman was in conflict with the claims of the head of the household, rather than making prescriptions for Christian families. She outlines the way in which Christianity became polarized, so that the elements of it which challenged family and state were expressed on the margins in the monastic communities, while mainstream Christianity set about Christianizing the patriarchal family and the state in the form of the Roman Empire. Hierarchical patterns of power in the family and the state, far from being transformed by the Christian vision, were made sacred; and the Church became locked into a role as defender of traditional family life – something it is increasingly called upon to enact today.

Notes

1. S. Grunlan, quoted in P. Pothan, *Unpackaging the Family* (Nottingham, Grove Books, 1992), p.13.

2. W. Clark, in L. Segal, ed., *What Is to Be Done About the Family?* (Harmondsworth, Penguin, 1983), p. 189.

3. B. Appleby, quoted in Y. Roberts, *Mad About Women* (London, Virago, 1992), p. 116.

4. S. Walrond-Skinner, *The Fulcrum and the Fire* (London, Darton, Longman & Todd, 1993), p. 97.

5. Pothan, *Unpackaging the Family*, p. 11.

6. See W. Seccombe, *Weathering the Storm* (London, Verso, 1993).

7. The Lambeth Conference, *The Truth Shall Make You Free* (1988), p. 186, emphasis added.

8. H. Anderson, *The Family and Pastoral Care* (Philadelphia, Fortress Press, 1984), p. 15. This is also an emphasis found in Walrond-Skinner's work.

9. D. Gittins, *The Family in Question* (London, Macmillan, 1993 [1985]), p. 10.

10. In the early 1990s, 21 per cent of adults were cohabiting in the south, excluding London, 16-18 per cent in London, the East Midlands, Yorkshire and Humberside, 7 per cent in Wales, and 11-14 per cent in the rest of England and Scotland.

11. See also D. Eversley and L. Bonnerjea, 'Social change and indications of diversity', in R. N. Rapoport, M. Fogarty, and R. Rapoport, eds, *Families in Britain* (London, Routledge & Kegan

Paul, 1982). Though over ten years old, this article still usefully illustrates the variety of family experience across different parts of the country.

12. The illegitimacy rate was also high. It has been suggested that nearly two-thirds of pregnancies occurred outside wedlock in this period, though it is hard to track down exact figures. See C. Rogers and J. Smith, *Local Family History in England* (Manchester, Manchester University Press, 1991).

13. O. R. Johnston, *Who Needs the Family?* (Illinois, IVP, 1979), p. 69.

14. G. Murdock, *Social Structure* (New York, Macmillan, 1949).

15. F. Edholm, 'The Unnatural Family', in E. Whitelegg et al., eds, *The Changing Experience of Women* (Oxford, Martin Robertson, 1982).

16. In *The Family in Question*. Gittins estimates that only 10 per cent of marriages across the world are actually monogamous, since polygamy, polyandry, and serial marriage are so common.

17. A. Ortlund, *Disciplines of the Home* (Milton Keynes, Word UK, 1990), p. 14.

18. S. Barton, 'Towards a Theology of the Family', *Crucible*, January-March 1993, p. 9.

19. J. Rogerson, *Institute for the Study of Christianity and Sexuality Bulletin*, no. 9, Spring 1993, p. 3.

20. R. Anderson and D. Guernsey, *On Being Family* (Michigan, William B. Eerdmans, 1985). I have to say that while this book is an important attempt to do some serious theology about family, the language is often convoluted and technical, and it is not very accessible for the general reader.

21. B. Friedan, *The Feminine Mystique* (Harmondsworth, Penguin Books, 1963).

22. See K. Barth, *Church Dogmatics*, III Vol. 4 (Edinburgh, T. & T. Clark, 1961).

23. For example, see J. Dominian, *Passionate and Compassionate Love* (London, Darton, Longman & Todd, 1991).

24. Barton, 'Towards a Theology of the Family', p. 11.

25. Johnston, *Who Needs the Family?*, p. 143.

26. R. Ruether, 'Church and Family in the Scriptures and Early Christianity', *New Blackfriars,* vol. 1, January 1984, p. 6.

chapter four

The Moral Minority

What society most desperately needs from the churches today is a clear, definite, and repeated statement of personal morality.

Douglas Hurd[1]

To proclaim family without grappling with the real dilemmas of a sinful world would not be strong leadership. It would be a cop-out.

George Carey, Archbishop of Canterbury[2]

Great God, in Christ you call our name,
And then receive us as your own,
Not through some merit, right or claim,
But by your gracious love alone.
We strain to glimpse your mercy seat
And find you kneeling at our feet.

Brian Wren[3]

Families continue to manage as best they can, family form is changing, but it is 'The Family' as an ideological and theological construct which is at the centre of the moral crisis. What happens to that construct has some effect on the other two understandings of family as kith and kin, and of family as household; but it gets in the way of reaching a proper understanding of what is going on in family life today. This is partly because the idea of 'The Family' has been misused for ideological and political ends, but also because it has become a symbol for many other values.

55

'Family' as symbol

Alexandra Artley suggested in the old *Sunday Correspondent* a few years ago that 'the family' is a form of shorthand which women in particular use to describe their general happiness, and the kind of society in which they want to live. It means 'proper care for the sick, poor and old; fairness and respect towards women as mothers and workers, even long-term "nurturing" projects such as state education and the environment. For women voters, "the family" really means the social agenda.' That probably applies to men too, for most of us see the family as larger than life, symbolic of something important, regardless of whether we love or hate our own kin, and the term 'family values' represents all of that. Anything that seems to threaten family life threatens the possibility of love, security, and happiness in general, so it is hard to be entirely objective about it.[4]

Through the industrial era, the family came to be seen as the place where the proletariat could realize personal identity, and as a last refuge from capitalism. Still today, for many men especially, the family is seen as a haven from the harsh world of work – though it is a little odd to think it can be both a refuge from society and a cornerstone of it. Friedan suggests that if the family is seen as the final frontier of privacy and autonomy, any perceived threat to it, like women's emancipation, imperils basic human values. The family, for both sexes, says Friedan, 'is the symbol of that last area where one has any hope of individual control over one's destiny, of meeting one's most basic human needs, of nourishing that core of personhood'.[5] It is true that many families do provide warmth, a sense of belonging, security, and a sense of self. But the symbolic value of 'The Family' survives – despite the evidence not only that many families are far from being havens, but that violence and abuse against women and children have been sanctioned as acceptable in the patriarchal family. For Christians, 'The Family' also represents the place where one can be Christian, and this too has historical roots, as I indicated earlier. The role of the Church in society has come to be seen essentially as a guardian of private morality, and, amidst all the talk of family values, the Church has been regarded as a key player.

Bring on the Church of England

For some, the Church has already failed. The *Daily Express*, launching its moral crusade early in 1993, accused it of having lost its stomach for its traditional role as 'the prime repository and teacher of moral values'. Instead of condemning wickedness, church leaders were busy talking about the ozone layer and monetary policy. So, said the *Express*, with a touching faith in the morality and integrity of our elected politicians, government ministers should lead the fight against moral breakdown.[6] None the less, there were many who believed the Church did have a role to play. As one *Guardian* journalist wrote: 'Like scurrying beetles under an upturned stone in the sunlight, the people of the Church are finding that their message is suddenly relevant. They are in demand. A moral void has opened up in society and there is nobody to fill it but George Carey!'[7] References to the Church tend to be, like this one, strictly about the Church of England, and to ignore other denominations – although the Catholic Church is sometimes included. This means that much of the thorough work done by the Free Churches receives no publicity, which is a loss. Similarly, other faiths have much to contribute, but are rarely called on to provide a moral perspective.[8] However, the role the Church of England is called to play on traditional morality and family values raises important issues which need to be examined.

In July 1992, the General Synod of the Church of England debated a motion on cohabitation, which originally requested its House of Bishops to 'give moral guidance to the nation concerning the nature of Christian Marriage today' in the light of the increase in cohabitation. It was not carried in this form, but the debate generated was an interesting one. Was it the Church of England's role to give a moral lead to the nation, and how could this be done effectively? Is it ever possible to teach people to be moral simply by lecturing them? Should there be an emphasis on holding out firm moral principles of right and wrong, or on caring for people in the situations they are actually in? The debate appears to have been a surprisingly good one, with a lot of openness and understanding, principally because so many Synod members had experience of cohabitation in their families. Whether or not we agree that a House of Bishops is the most appropriate vehicle for giving moral guidance, it is to them that many people look rather than to the synodical process or theologians in general. Even those outside the Church of England may believe that its House of Bishops has a particular responsibility to speak out about personal morality.

In an article in the London *Evening Standard* in December 1992, nicely headed 'Who will rid us of this bland twaddle?', Stephen Glover castigated Church of England bishops for not being outspoken about the evils of divorce at the time that the separation of the Prince and Princess of Wales was announced. They 'shrink from making moral pronouncements', he says, 'the laity decides how it wishes to behave and then looks to its timorous religious leaders to offer justification. . . . it does not expect to be criticised or condemned.' Glover looks back to the good old days when Anglican bishops were terrifying figures who fixed you with a beady eye and took a firm moral line.[9] Glover wants bishops to tell us what is right and wrong so that we know, even if we take not the slightest bit of notice. For him, that is the point of an established Church, and many people share that view. It's as if people can be quite happy doing as they wish, as long as they know *someone* (in this case the Church of England) will look after the moral standards for them, so that society doesn't lose them altogether.

Taking a firm line

It is true that it is important in many areas of life to know what the boundaries of behaviour are. Children, for example, need to have limits set against which they can then test themselves, and perhaps rebel. If they are allowed to do absolutely anything, they feel lost, and may behave outrageously in an attempt to be controlled. Someone who takes up a new post probably won't find it helpful to be told, 'just do it your way'. People actually need to be told how things have usually been done, so that they know what norm they are departing from. So it may be right that people and communities need to have some sense of norms against which they can judge their own beliefs and behaviour. In that case, it is useful to have a Church which is clear about what is helpful and what is harmful for human flourishing.

As in parenting, any limits that are set have to be realistic and explainable, and some of them may change over time. Some rules will be absolute, and with some there can be flexibility. The Church of England, like other churches, is having to think through whether some of its traditional rules are still applicable – and that is a useful process to go through even if no changes are thought necessary in the end. One difficulty is that in times of trouble and unsettling change, people have a great desire to hold on to traditional rules. Order, stability, and continuity are highly valued. Clearly they do have importance; the stories and doctrines found in Christian tradition offer guidance for the future as well as lessons from the past. That tradition, though, has always been dynamic and open to change. The necessity to be firm in upholding those things that are central to the gospel should not be confused with inflexibility. Much that is said by Christians on family issues falls into that trap, and we are in danger of insisting on absolutes which lead not to human flourishing but to a new legalism.

This is partly because it is not easy doing your thinking under the close and critical scrutiny of a world that thinks in headlines. What Glover seems to be arguing is that it doesn't much matter *what* bishops say, as long as they say something decisive. It is better to be strong but wrong, than to be thoughtful. It is much harder for the media to deal with thoughtfulness than to have something hard-line to set up and attack (or praise) – for example, the press could deal with the Pope reaffirming opposition to contraception, simply by bringing on lots of commentators to say how out of touch this was. But there also seems to be a feeling in our society that not to have immediate answers is to be 'wishy-washy' and worthy of ridicule. It is interesting to see how John Major worked hard to escape the label 'ditherer' applied to him in the early months of his premiership, by trying to be forthright – condemning more and understanding less. It is as if the nation cannot tolerate any leader of Church or state who values the weighing up of issues before taking action.

George Carey did try to take a thoughtful approach, as his article in the *Daily Mail*, quoted earlier, illustrates. But there has been a detectable trend towards bishops and other church leaders making more forceful statements, and often receiving disproportionate media coverage for doing so. There is of course a place for sharp definite statements, rather than always using the 'on the one hand this, on the other hand that' formula. However, they must spring from a proper analysis of issues, serious theological thinking and, perhaps above all, sympathetic care for people caught up in a situation. There is a constant tension in the Church between the desire for a firm moral line and the rather messy complex situations people are actually in. How do you place absolutes about the sanctity of life against the pain of parents who cannot mourn a son kept alive in a persistent vegetative state? How do you balance a public moral denunciation of cohabitation with the effect on couples who might be approaching the Church for marriage at a very significant moment in their relationship? If such couples meet condemnation, or are required to go through a public repentance as some churches insist, they may be driven away from God and the Church altogether. Richard Harries comments that moral exhortation by itself is not enough, for 'dry bone morality' does not point us to the vision of God. Rather, he comments: 'Aware of our own failings and willing to accept other people despite theirs, the church seeks to be a community of mutual acceptance rooted in the forgiveness of God.'[10]

This is the major theme of Peter Selby's book *BeLonging*. For him, the vital point is that we are made members of the church family by adoption, not by any qualifications of blood or merit. This should mean that we reject all attempts at exclusiveness, which allows some to be full members of Christ's Church, but excommunicates others. For this reflects not the true family of God, but a narrow tribalism. He illustrates this theme with descriptions of the way the Church of England has dealt with ordaining women as priests, with gay and lesbian people, and with ethnic minorities. The Church must be open and welcoming to all who would be part of it, however uncomfortable this may be, and we need to remember that those who most seem strangers in our midst may be bringing new insights. He argues that although there may be some practices so alien to the Church's life that there must be exclusion, this must only be a last resort, for we follow one who was himself a victim of exclusion:

> A Church founded on unmerited and unconstrained mercy may not at times be the Church we would like; but it is the only Church we have been given. It may fail to guarantee our proud entitlements or protect our vulnerabilities; but it is the only kind of Church that could make space for the new life, the rejected perceptions or the unexpected love on which our shared future depends.[11]

Interfering in politics

I shall return to these issues in later chapters. However, it is interesting to note that the desire for the Church to give a firm moral lead evaporates when the matters in question are those of social policy – though I would also want to argue that what are seen as matters of personal, private morality are actually also about social policy and societal attitudes. There is much less willingness to accept the Church giving a clear moral lead by condemning injustice. Faced with a couple, royal or any other, whose marriage is in difficulties, and who want to divorce, many would have the Church make clear statements about divorce being wrong, rather than showing compassion and understanding and helping them to find a way forward together or apart. Faced with people begging on the streets, the Church may be urged to take a non-judgemental pastorally caring line, but definitely *not* to take a moral line – unless it is to denounce some select categories of undeserving poor. Feeding and caring for homeless people, whatever the cause of their situation, is seen as admirable (look at the regard in which Mother Teresa is held). But denouncing society, or calling particular pieces of social policy immoral if they contribute to homelessness, is thought to be outside the Church's brief – it is not for the Church to 'interfere in politics'.

And again, whereas in the area of personal morality the Church is asked to make uncompromising statements, being forthright in the wider sphere is condemned. Bishops who make sharp comments about social policy are told they are too simplistic or naive. There was some interesting discussion in the *Sunday*

Express following a television interview with John Habgood, in which he made some critical comment on the competitive spirit engendered by Conservatives, and linked crime with hopelessness and unemployment: 'I'm not saying people aren't bad, but often the badness is brought out of them by circumstances . . . crime, particularly . . . in young people, arises out of a sense that "we have no stake in society" . . . The Government, with its strong emphasis on competitive success, feeds the notion that in our society . . . we are against each other.'

The *Sunday Express* published reactions from some Tory MPs, who said things like: 'Why doesn't he tackle some of the more important moral issues, like having children out of wedlock, rather than the easy political ones?' And 'The Church should get on with spiritual guidance and leave economics to the politicians.' Another said: 'His comments are easy to make from the unreal world of the cathedral cloister.' Whether or not we agree with Habgood's analysis, it's a strange view of Christianity which lies behind the criticisms. Why is the unreal world of the cathedral cloister acceptable for commenting on sex outside marriage and for offering spiritual guidance? Doesn't it matter being irrelevant here? An editorial then attacked the Church and Habgood in particular for failing the nation: individual goodness and wickedness 'permeate almost every page of the Bible', but Habgood chooses to speak about unemployment. The biblical themes of mercy, compassion, and forgiveness are clearly not part of the *Express*'s theology. For it, John Major's dictum that society should 'condemn a little more and understand a little less' is much more on the right lines: 'If individuals and communities were to do more condemning, the courts would eventually do less convicting.'

The next day, however, the *Express* launched a crusade to campaign for good citizens, and approvingly quoted Cardinal Basil Hume saying much the same as John Habgood had said. Clearly, it is the Church of England which should not be 'meddling' in politics, whereas other denominations don't matter as much – which is rather odd given that the Church of England has seats by right in the House of Lords. Is it that the only political role allowed the Church of England is to be a Department of Private Morality, but that it should not interfere in any other areas? If so, establishment is acting to limit its role in politics, rather than enhancing it. There is a great danger here of the Church allowing itself to be used for political purposes. As Gittins points out, the greatest moral concern over illegitimacy and single mothers occurs where a state's finances are concerned. This was true with the Poor Laws of both Elizabethan and Victorian times, and is true today: 'the main reason for the stigmatisation of illegitimacy in Western Europe has been economic. Neither parish nor state has ever wanted to be financially responsible for children without social fathers, and hence the harsh treatment of unmarried mothers.' Thus today, it is the single mothers on welfare who are most severely criticized, not the divorced partners of MPs. Writes Gittins: 'so long as people did not become either a financial liability to the State or a threat to social and political order, despite the plethora of middle-class moralising, governments cared (and care) very little as to the actual living arrangements people entered into in order to survive.'[12] Excitement that the Church is in demand should not blind us to the limits of what we are being asked to do.

Resisting privatization

The Church as a whole has to reject being privatized, as Susan Dowell comments in *They Two Shall Be One*. The idea that Christians should not be conformed to the world, she says, is usually understood as meaning we must uphold Christian standards on subjects like sexuality over against the permissive secular world. However, Dowell points out that refusing to be conformed to the world in our day means resisting the attempt to place the Church entirely in the domestic sphere, 'from which it is required to guard the nation's private purity, while leaving the nation undisturbed in its "real" business'.[13] We have accepted far too easily the idea that the Church's place is in the private realm of personal relationships, and that speaking out on poverty, unemployment, education, or whatever needs special justification. It is often said that we live in a pluralistic society, yet – as Brian Walsh points out in *Third Way* magazine – there is one overarching belief in our culture: it is that beliefs are simply a matter of personal choice and that faith commitments are private decisions separable from public life. Christians need to insist (as will other faith communities) that faith and its associated world view is integral to all of life, not a private matter of personal devotion in special institutions. The Christian community needs to 'demonstrate through our life together and through our political, economic, educational, ecclesiastical, and other cultural activities that the gospel is indeed good news for all of life'.[14]

Following this course should not, however, mean being assimilated by the culture in which the Church finds itself. There are still those who look back to a time when the Church was a real socio-political and cultural force, though it is questionable whether the gospel it was demonstrating was that of Jesus Christ, or the 'god of mammon with its associated motifs of conquest, violence and control'. Those who think this way 'hate the fact that Christians are now on the margins of mainstream society', notes Walsh, but 'The radical reformers would tell us that the church should always be on the margins – and . . . they are right.'[15] In its earliest days, Christianity was seen as being subversive both towards the state and the family. It may be that we need to recapture the vision of a radical minority Christian community rather than trying to win recognition of the Church as a Department of Personal Morality.

The fact that we live in troublous times must not lead us into moral panic, or to retreat into our own private world. The message of the Christian gospel about the mercy, compassion and love of God is needed more than ever, and must be lived out in the day-to-day witness of Christians as well as in the public comments of the Church. If public comments are to be made about family life, they must be grounded in an understanding of what is really going on – not just looking at the statistics, but understanding where the pressure points are for real people. That is what the rest of this book is about.

Notes

1. D. Hurd, quoted in M. Brake and C. Hale, *Public Order and Private Lives* (London, Routledge, 1992), p. 87.

2. George Carey, *Daily Mail*, 2 August 1993.

3. B. Wren, 'Great God, your love has called us here'.

4. A. Artley, *Sunday Correspondent*, 19 November 1989.

5. B. Friedan, *The Second Stage* (New York, Summit Books, 1981), p. 229.

6. The government's subsequent stress on morality, and its 'back to basics' campaign, somewhat backfired in early 1994 when some of its own ministers were revealed to be behaving immorally. The moral element of 'back to basics' rather got played down after this.

7. Quoted in the *Church Times*, April 1993.

8. Jewish thinkers do have a slightly higher profile. The Inner Cities Religious Council is one attempt to draw together different faiths to address social situations.

9. No doubt some did – and some still do – but it probably wasn't true for the majority of them. What is interesting is the desire many people have for stern authority figures. Cf. the *Express*'s reference to 'the stern, confident moral teaching of the Church' in former days.

10. R. Harries, *The Times*, 20 March 1993.

11. P. Selby, *BeLonging* (London, SPCK, 1991), p. 78.

12. D. Gittins, *The Family in Question* (London, Macmillan, 1993 [1985]), pp. 106 and 142.

13. S. Dowell, *They Two Shall Be One* (London, Collins, 1990), p. xi.

14. B. Walsh, in *Third Way*, Summer 1992, p. 29.

15. Walsh, *Third Way*, p. 27.

chapter five

Living Together,
Living Apart

*Marriage . . . is never a contract between equals, since
men and women are not equals.*

Christine Delphy and Diana Leonard[1]

*Marriage, as an unconditional commitment, imposes the
limitations that make a creative relationship possible, just
as form provides the essential boundaries and structure
for the creative act.*

Madonna Kolbenschlag[2]

*When the Church appears to forget that morality is about
people and their joys and sorrows and what is truly good
for them, it is no wonder that so many of our con-
temporaries expect no understanding from the Church,
either of what makes them happy, their hopes and plans,
or of what they fear and what worries and miseries they
are going through.*

Helen Oppenheimer[3]

The current concern over family life is largely related to what
adult couples do: how they set up their relationships, and who
with, and what happens when those relationships break down.
What happens to children caught up in broken adult relationships
needs special attention, yet what childless couples do has an effect
on the stability of marriage in general, and the expectations placed
on it. In this chapter, I want to look at cohabitation, divorce, and
marriage, and their effect on family life, and more generally at the

values which underlie the Church's response. My main focus will be on heterosexual relationships, which are the basis of the vast majority of family arrangements, though gay and lesbian partnerships will be a part of the picture.

Cohabitation

The increase in cohabitation has led many to question whether there is any future for marriage – and they fear that any collapse in marriage will bring ruin to family life and therefore to society. Yet as Dormer points out, 'as things stand at present, the majority of the population in virtually all Western European countries still marry at some time in their lives, so that we must exercise caution in predicting its demise'.[4] Also, it is far from clear that co-habitation is a direct threat to marriage, since some three-quarters of those who cohabit do marry in the end. Although in some cases people drift into cohabitation, or do so as a result of housing difficulties, moving in together is generally a significant step in a serious relationship which does not wish for either the extended commitment or the perceived restrictions of marriage. On average, about half of all couples getting married in England and Wales will have lived together first, though this ranges from around a quarter of couples cohabiting before first marriages, to around three-quarters for subsequent ones. There is also a geographical variation – Scotland and Wales, for example, have half the cohabitation levels of England.

Cohabitation is a topic which generates a lot of concern amongst Christians, particularly among the middle-aged whose own children are cohabiting. Dealing with the public face of children's sexuality is not always easy at any age. And cohabitation can raise complex feelings in people who grew up believing that sex was for marriage – all that self-control or guilt over *our* lapses, and now everybody does it! The issue is often dealt with through the 'NIMBB syndrome' – 'I realize you are sleeping together, but Not In My Back Bedroom'! Many Christians acknowledge, however, that there is a great deal of difference between promiscuity, and being sexually intimate in a long-term, committed relationship. A cohabiting couple who are committed to an exclusive, permanent, faithful relationship are often said to be fulfilling the conditions of marriage, even though they have not gone through a ceremony. Karl Barth observes that, 'Two people may be formally married and fail to live a life which can seriously be regarded as married life. And it may happen that two people are not married and yet in their precarious way live under the law of marriage. A wedding is only the regulative confirmation and legitimation of a marriage before and by society. It does not constitute marriage.'[5] It is important to continue to place a high value on sexual intimacy, and to say that the context within which it is experienced matters. But rather than condemning those who cohabit as sexually irresponsible, Christians need to ask why it happens, and what this says about marriage.

I would like to comment briefly on four factors which seem to be involved, for they raise important issues.[6]

1. A trial marriage

Young people have seen the increase in divorce since 1960, and may well have suffered when their parents' marriage broke down. Therefore they decide to have a trial marriage, in order to avoid divorce in the future. Also, people who have already been through marriage and divorce are much more likely to cohabit – both because they may be waiting for a divorce to come through, and because they feel more reluctant to commit themselves to marriage again after a bad experience. Unfortunately, a relationship which works when cohabiting does not always work later on in marriage. Relate counsellors report that couples do not expect things to change if they get married, but it is actually a much bigger step than they anticipate, and this can cause problems. Recent figures suggest that couples who have cohabited are *more* likely to divorce than those who have not. However, it is not possible to tell whether it is *because* they have cohabited that they run into problems, or some other cause.

2. Equality

Women feel more equal with their partners if they cohabit, whereas marriage institutionalizes inequality between the sexes. The agony column in my local paper had an example of this from a woman who wrote:

I lived with my boyfriend for four years before we married. . . . Since we married my husband's attitude has changed towards me. Before the wedding he would help me to get breakfast, now he sits and waits for me to make the coffee and butter the toast. Our sex life was great before we married. Now I feel as if my husband is exercising his rights as a husband when we make love.[7]

In fact, cohabiting relationships may still be unequal, but the inequality is less institutionalized.

Models of marriage based on what was seen in the parental home can get superimposed on the relationship – even when a couple have been living together for some time. This often means that partners take on particular roles as husband and wife, where the husband is the breadwinner with little domestic responsibility, and the wife makes a home, nurtures the children, and perhaps also contributes extras to the family income. This idea, strongly set out in sociological thinking in the 1950s to 1970s, still influences people's perceptions of marriage, even though it is inadequate and restrictive.[8] The young women in Ann Phoenix's discussion of young mothers were not very positive about marriage, and felt cohabitation had fewer disadvantages. Although the majority thought they would marry at some point, they felt it restricted women's freedom, and they disliked the drudgery associated with women's traditional roles in marriage.[9]

Some women make a deliberate choice not to marry for these reasons. *Woman's Hour* presenter Jenni Murray speaks of marriage as a trap, with 'centuries of tradition . . . pushing you into a preordained role – a submissive one of helpmeet, carer, servant. Women can find independence in or out of a relationship if they choose to eschew that band of gold'.[10] Many feminists are particularly critical of marriage and family life for this reason, and some see the nuclear family as an instrument of oppressive social control. Thus Delphy and Leonard argue that 'domestic groups are . . . primarily . . . part of a system of labour relations in which men benefit from, and exploit, the work of women – and sometimes that of their children and other male relatives too.'[11]

Church teaching as well as marriage and social security laws reinforce those roles. However, there have been significant changes in the law regarding women's position within marriage. There is now a mutual right of support, rather than it being assumed that husbands must support their wives, for instance. But assumptions are still made about women's status – for example, the married couple's tax allowance in Britain must generally be paid to the husband. It is still expected that women will change their surname on marriage, although a few do not. Some Christians would want to argue that if couples followed biblical ideas about male headship, far fewer marriages would break down. Others would suggest that if the Church offered a supportive theology of equal partnership in marriage, more couples would want to get married and stay married. I shall return to this point later.

3. The rejection of celibacy

The average age for marriage is the late twenties, and abstinence from sexual activity until that age seems impossible, especially as people are now reaching sexual maturity early in their teens. Despite occasional affirmations of the value of celibacy in a world threatened by AIDS, it is still very likely that a couple who are in love and intending to spend their future together will be sexually intimate. If the Church is concerned to uphold the value of keeping sex for marriage, then such a couple would need to be encouraged to marry young, to avoid years of temptation. However, it is youthful marriages which are most likely to break down. The couple who marry when they are mature are much more likely to have a lasting marriage. If we value the permanency of marriage, we need to discourage people from marrying young. Christians have to do some hard thinking about whether the emphasis should be on upholding the permanence of marriage, or keeping people celibate until marriage. Accepting cohabitation may be the price that needs to be paid for safeguarding the permanence of marriage.

In fact, there is precedent for the Church being less rigid about sex outside marriage. Sex before marriage was accepted by the Church in the Middle Ages. A betrothal would take place, the couple would live together, and only marry if the woman proved fertile. The Church's blessing was not originally seen as the inauguration of marriage, but the confirmation of it, since marriage began with the private mutual consent of the partners before two witnesses. It was not until 1753 that Church and state in England insisted that a marriage, to be recognized, had to be performed in public – though whether this had much effect on ordinary people's liaisons is questionable. A number of Christians suggest we need some way of registering a union which does not require the same firm commitment of marriage in church or register office. Jack Spong, for example, in his book *Living in Sin*,[12] advocates the Church formalizing a betrothal ceremony for engaged couples, which would not be as binding as marriage. I am not sure how this would work since one reason couples cohabit is that they do not want the formal, public commitment. Butterworth suggests a kind of civil marriage which is less than a full Christian ceremony, but more than informal cohabitation.[13] Oppenheimer is critical of this kind of idea, saying that there are dangers with any approach which distinguishes between Christian marriage and a secular kind, for marriage is not the special preserve of believers.[14]

4. Love is private

There has been a decrease in religious practice, and young people are sceptical that a piece of paper or ceremony makes any difference if they love each other. It may be too that the breakdown of the idea of society is also implicated. Getting married is a public commitment to each other, taken before witnesses, and requiring a legal process for its undoing. Yet if the trend over the last fourteen years has been that 'there is no such thing as society', there may seem little point in making a statement to it about a private relationship. The culture has been to attack bureaucracy and red tape, and perhaps it should not be surprising that marriage as a formal institution is not highly regarded in this climate. Some couples who do decide to get married, keep the whole thing very quiet. It is seen as something private between the two of them, and a few of them do not even tell anybody. Having said that, many cohabiting couples do go on to get married, and some want a big ceremony to mark the occasion. The financial expense of doing this may be one reason why they wait to get married.

The increase in cohabitation shows not so much that committed relationships are under threat, as that the institution of marriage is viewed differently. In some respects it is taken more seriously than in the past, with couples taking their time before going into it, and the majority of marriages do still last until the death of one partner. In fact, the average length of a marriage is longer today than it was a hundred years ago (at around thirty years compared with twenty-eight back in the 1890s), since people live longer. In other respects, marriage is a creaky institution which is regarded as hindering good relationships rather than allowing them to flourish. We need to know much more about what makes relationships work, and look at how Christian teaching about marriage can foster its success.

Changed meanings for marriage

Reliable contraception, relative affluence, and the education and emancipation of women have changed the meaning of marriage, so that today we most frequently see it as being about love, and providing a loving environment in which to raise children if we have them. A study of European values found that when asked what made a successful marriage, 85 per cent of respondents rated mutual respect, appreciation, and faithfulness highly; 80 per cent highly rated understanding and tolerance; a happy sexual relationship was important for 64 per cent; and children were important for 59 per cent. This contrasts with attitudes in the 1950s, when couples stressed that fulfilment of the homemaker and breadwinner roles were necessary for a happy marriage, and income and housing were seen as important.

The Churches too have moved in their understandings of marriage, so that they share the secular view. The Catholic Church in particular has become more positive about seeing marriage as a vocation of equal value with celibacy. And it has moved away from speaking of procreation as the primary end of marriage, with 'mutual help' and the 'relief of concupiscence' (sexual desire) as a secondary end. Now the talk is much more of the importance of personal love and intimacy between the couple reflecting Christ's love. The Church of England's Alternative Service Book states that marriage is given that 'husband and wife may comfort and help each other, living faithfully together . . . that they may know each other in love . . . through joy of their bodily union . . . and they may have children and be blessed in caring for them'. Its report *Marriage and the Church's Task* goes further and speaks of it as 'a relational bond of personal love, a compound of commitment, experience and response, in which the commitment clothes itself in the flesh and blood of a living union'.[15]

One of the most influential proponents of this modern Christian view of marriage is Jack Dominian. In *Passionate and Compassionate Love*, he describes the way in which secular and theological views of marriage come together to see marriage and family as a community of love. Because most Western families now have good shelter and material provisions, people are seeking emotional and sexual fulfilment. Marriage primarily offers healing and wholeness, and continuity, stability, and reliability are necessary for that to happen. Marriages like this have to be worked at, not abandoned when difficulties appear, although divorce may need to be a possibility in some circumstances. The reason sex belongs in marriage is that 'its authentic meaning can only be experienced within the context of a continuous, reliable and predictable relationship which is usually marriage'. Dominian argues that the rise in divorce 'is due to a rapid transformation from task-orientated togetherness to a personal, emotional encounter which needs different education, social skills and support'.[16]

Similarly, Butterworth believes that men and women are so damaged emotionally and spiritually by the time they reach adulthood, that 'their capacity to give and receive love freely and openly has been severely curtailed'. But, he claims, God's intention is that each of us should find the unconditional love which can heal us within marriage, and that this will in turn lead us to knowing God as the source of all love. Love of this kind can start its healing process before marriage, but marriage is necessary as a safeguard 'to ensure that both man and wife are committed to the healing of their partner as well as to receiving healing for themselves'.[17] Clearly, this is an understanding of marriage that only makes sense for societies where other, physical needs are met, and thus cannot be God's universal intention for marriage. However, it is quite reasonable to suppose that God can work in marriage in different ways according to its meaning in a particular society. We should not assume that there is one universal style of

'Christian marriage' which has universal characteristics. Even in the affluent West, not everyone will look to marriage to provide emotional healing. Bonds which meet some of these deeper needs may be built with other relations or friends, with marriage offering economic security, or a parenting partnership. Moreover, the vision of marriage as emotional healing can come to seem hollow if a couple become parents. There are inevitable tensions between the partners' needs in relation to each other, and the demands of raising children. Marriage is sustained through this phase of life not by a romantic vision, but by commitment and friendship – and oases of intimacy when the children stay with relatives!

The idea of marriage as a place where people know one another's wounds and can offer healing, has further difficulties in that the current state of play between the sexes makes it all but impossible for this new vision to work. We are ill-equipped to sustain a dynamic relationship of loving intimacy for forty or fifty years, and marriage may be the place where wounds are inflicted and reopened rather than healed. Those who describe marriage in this way are clear that it is a two-way process, in which both men and women minister to one another. Yet given the difficulty many men have with emotional expression, the reality is that many women provide emotional nurturing for men, without receiving much in return. Men and women often operate with different perceptions of the world, as Deborah Tannen shows, and may struggle to understand one another's priorities.[18] The inequalities of marriage are one reason why it seems irrelevant or oppressive to many women. Unless the new perception of marriage as an equal nurturing partnership takes into account what has gone before, and understands the present reality of gender relations for most people, it will simply be irrelevant. The Church as a whole needs to listen more closely to feminist and structural analyses of what marriage is, if its marital theology is to be rooted in reality.

An interesting consequence of the concentration on marriage as healing and emotional fulfilment, is that it makes it more difficult to condemn gay and lesbian partnerships which have the same characteristics. If marriage is not primarily about procreation, but about providing a framework of permanency within which individuals may become intimate and minister to one another, the same features can apply. Churches are still in a state of flux over homosexuality as an issue, but it is interesting that the Church of England bishops recognized the possibilities of healing in faithful homosexual partnerships, and found it difficult to condemn them outright for this reason.[19]

Bringing marriage down to earth

Though marriage breakdown is high, and relationships between the sexes generally fail to meet expectations, most people still look to marriage as the primary source for the lasting and fulfilling intimacy which they crave. Yet the very expectation that marriage will meet emotional needs may be one reason why marriage fails. If the chief value of marriage is emotional healing, it is impossible to tell people they must stay in a marriage and make it work. We cannot force one person to love, cherish, and heal another, whereas society can insist that they fulfil their duties to be responsible parents or breadwinners. Yet stressing duty makes marriage seem more like a loss of independence, and less desirable.

Perhaps one difficulty is that it is not so much marriage but romantic love which is seen as providing this emotional fulfilment, yet that kind of intense passion inevitably changes shape over time. People may seek to recapture such emotional excitement through extra-marital affairs, and adultery by women as well as men is fairly commonplace. Perhaps it deserves more attention by Christians, for adultery often causes great distress. It nearly always represents a betrayal of trust, and can leave scars even when the marriage continues. Unfortunately, the more comfortable, companionable love and affection that maintains good marriages often comes across as dull and respectable rather than fulfilling. Marriage is seen as providing the happy ending for a romance, but it can precisely feel like an ending. People have settled down, and are stuck for life. 'Till death us do part' marriage does not have a very positive image; it looks like a life sentence rather than fun. The end result, distorted by ageism, is posing cosily for the local paper after fifty years of marriage, with a lifetime's experience of a relationship reduced to platitudes: ' "The secret of a happy marriage is to keep smiling", says Annie, 76'. We need to recapture the sense of marriage as the beginning of a journey, in which partners can grow, and learn together how to make it work. This is something which may be appreciated more where marriages are arranged, and love is expected to grow over the years spent together.[20]

The romantic view of marriage suggests couples need no interests apart from one another, yet the idea that one person alone can be all the other needs is a strange one. Christians base a strong view of marriage as coupledom on the idea of man and woman 'cleaving together' to become one flesh. But as I have already pointed out, this union took place within an extended family set-up, and was not expected to be self-sufficient. Indeed, support from the wider family and community is often helpful in sustaining marriage, and both friends and family can meet some of the emotional needs which an individual partner does not fulfil. It is a dangerous fallacy to assume that intimacy must mean that neither partner can function without the other, and yet this is often put forward as God's intention: that only in the complementarity of male and female do we become whole. Making marriage a self-sufficient relationship also represents an individualism which fails to see how marriage relationships are embedded in other networks.

Rather than colluding with this romantic view, Christians should be much clearer that marriage relationships are dynamic things, which inevitably go through periods of conflict and readjustment as well as times of love and intense joy. The ideal is not continuous happiness, but that through all the changes and chances of life, for better and worse, richer and poorer, in sickness and in health, through barren times and good, the partners stay committed to one another. An abusive relationship falls away from this ideal, but one in which there are sometimes days when the couple hate each other but remain committed, still fulfils it.

The impact of divorce

Clearly, however, an increasing number of marriages do not achieve even this more attainable ideal. Partners may be abusive, exploitative, have affairs, or become soul-destroyingly indifferent to one another. Around a half of all marriages end in divorce, and this has been the subject of much debate both within the Church and in society at large. There is evidence that some children suffer long-term effects both before and after their parents break up, and I shall discuss this later on. Adults often find divorce stressful too: Walrond-Skinner notes that couples experiencing divorce are six times more at risk of being hospitalized for mental disorders, have more car accidents, serious physical illnesses, and higher instances of alcoholism and substance abuse. They are twice as likely to commit suicide.

Because we expect so much of marriage, a divorce betrays our deepest aspirations, and leaves deep psychological scars that can take months or years to work through. Because so many of us have the experience of divorce, either for ourselves or amongst our family and friends, it is hard for us to accept that it might be a bad thing, for this seems to condemn what they have done. But unless we are able to look realistically at the consequences of divorce, we will not be able as a society to provide the support that is needed either to sustain marriage or to pick up the pieces when it ends. Dominian argues that marital and family breakdown should eclipse all other social issues for Christians, since it has such dire consequences. Society itself bears the cost of picking up the pieces, and meeting the increased demands for housing, health care, and child support. The current legal process for divorce in England and Wales is lengthy and costly, and fosters acrimonious battles over property and children. An emphasis on settling out of court using conciliation services seems to offer a better hope of minimizing the damage, and this has been part of recent discussion about reform of the divorce laws.

Equally, social policy is implicated in rising divorce rates – along with problems in relationships and changing expectations of marriage. The number of families on the poverty line (defined by the government as less than half average earnings) has trebled to 1.5 million since 1979, and financial worries can break up a marriage which might have survived in better circumstances. Stress within a family may cause parents to take out their anxieties on children, who then behave badly, and in turn add to the stress. However, Malcolm Wicks, former Director of the Family Policy Studies Centre, points out that the causes of divorce 'spring from fundamental social, economic and psychological developments that are occurring worldwide'. That no solution has been found 'is indicative of the power, and complexity, of the changes that we are experiencing'. None the less, he argues, Britain has not handled these family changes at all well.[21] And the divorce rate in the United Kingdom is one of the highest in Europe, though not yet as high as in the United States.

As with the rise in cohabitation, a key reason for the rise in divorce is the change in the social situation of women. To blame increasing divorce on the evils of feminism misreads what is actually happening, but there is a connection. Feminism has encouraged women not to put up with destructive relationships, and has made it more feasible for women to survive alone. Both in the United Kingdom and in other European countries, about 70 per cent of divorces are instigated by women. Some 55 per cent, the largest category, are granted on the grounds of the husband's unreasonable behaviour. The largest category for divorces initiated by men (44%) are on the grounds of female adultery. Men remarry quicker after divorce than women do. This may be because they get a sense of identity from marriage, or feel failures if they are divorced. There is evidence that married men are on the whole healthier than those who are unmarried (though the reverse is true for women). Men's earlier remarriage rate may also reflect the fact that they are already living with, or have started a second family with, another woman.

The evidence does suggest that women have more deep-rooted dissatisfactions with marriage than do men. Men may leave a marriage for a new relationship, but find in the end that it offers no more than their original marriage did. Dominian quotes some research which suggests that 50 per cent of men and 30 per cent of women regret their divorce.[22] The middle-aged man going through a mid-life crisis in which he puts his marriage under threat or goes off with a younger woman is a well-known figure. What does such men's questioning and searching for identity mean in relation to marriage and their relationships with women? Women who have invested everything in marriage and children are often in a poor state when they are left. Indeed, a key reason many continue in marriages which are not satisfying for them is that they will be economically disadvantaged if they leave, and that their children will suffer. One of the advantages in leaving which many speak of is the discovery of their own independence. In this sense, the rise in divorce also contributes to it, since women see that it is possible to be independent – even though it may mean hardship.

The most likely time in a marriage for a divorce to occur is between five and nine years – 27 per cent of divorces happen then. About 18 per cent of divorces happen between ten and fourteen years and 13 per cent between fifteen and nineteen years. Early breakdown may occur because a couple have had unreal expectations of marriage, or it may coincide with parenthood. A relationship based on fairly egalitarian principles can take a knock when a baby comes along, and the woman finds herself shouldering the main domestic burden. Those in social classes IV and V are four times more likely to divorce than those in other social classes. This may well be related to the fact that they are more likely to marry young, as well as being more likely to suffer financial pressures. Dormer observes that 'young people from disadvantaged backgrounds use marriage as a way out only to find that by marrying and having children when they are young, they further disadvantage themselves with respect to education and employment'.[23] Divorce later in marriage often represents a time when children are nearing maturity, and a couple are faced with being alone with a partner with whom they have lost touch.

In all considerations of the effects of divorce, it is concern for the children of any broken marriage which commands most attention. Various studies have been done on the effect of divorce on children, and several have pointed to long-term difficulties and trauma. There have been question marks about such studies. They have tended to compare children of divorced parents with those in stable two-parent homes, rather than with children in unhappy, two-parent homes. So it is hard to tell whether it is better for a child to be brought up by one parent than live with parents who are violent or abusive towards one another. It is also hard to isolate whether damage is caused by other factors associated with divorce, such as poverty, or by emotional factors. Also, there may be a difference between the effect on children today where divorce is common, and the effect on children in previous decades when there was more stigma attached to it. However, some current studies which try to control for these factors have come to similar conclusions.

Increasing evidence is emerging that children caught up in their parents' divorce are especially vulnerable to a number of risks. Changed economic circumstances play a part in this, since one-parent families are more likely to live in poverty. But this is not the whole story, since those whose parents remarry are as likely to do badly as those in one-parent homes. Nor is it simply being father- or mother-less, since children who lose a parent through death tend to do better than those whose parents split up. Martin Richards suggests that it is living with parents who are hostile towards one another which leaves scars. He points out that 'signs of disruptive and unhappy behaviour in children seem to appear before their parents part', though he still argues that, on balance, divorce may be worse for children than enduring an unhappy marriage – if only because divorce also brings poverty.[24] This theme is explored by Jim Conway in *Adult Children of Legal or Emotional Divorce.*[25] Though the book as a whole is rather limited in scope, he argues convincingly that children suffer from the same negative psychological consequences if their parents are emotionally divorced, that they do with legal divorce. It is the dysfunction of the relationship which causes the problems, not the actual divorce. In contrast to Richards, he argues that conflict-ridden intact families are more damaging for children than being in a stable family after divorce has occurred. The key issue for him is the need to put damaged relationships right to prevent either kind of divorce occurring.

We do know that in many cases children suffer long-term trauma as their parents split up, but it is clear that children do sometimes come through the experience and grow as a result of it. Barbara Tizard refers to studies of children who have suffered adverse early experiences, and comments that 'a sizeable proportion of children seem to escape without any adverse effects, even when they remain in an adverse environment throughout childhood. . . . Whether early experience determines later development depends on later events, which can maintain, amplify, or counteract the influence of early experience.' Our knowledge of what makes this difference is limited as yet, though there are some pointers.

Relationships with siblings and other children can provide vital emotional support, as can having a positive stable link with grandparents or other relatives and friendly adults. Tizard points out that one study showed that a close relationship with a grandparent tended to protect children from the ill-effects of a disharmonious parental marriage.[26]

It is very difficult to know what is best in individual circumstances where relationships have broken down, and whether divorce may be the gateway to a happier future or a worse one. It is also difficult to balance the needs of individual families with the interests of society in encouraging stable marriage. It would seem reasonable that more effort be put into preventing relationships breaking down, and in offering help to families in crisis, so that damage can be minimized.[27] Counselling which helps partners to understand what has happened to them may sometimes allow a relationship to be mended, or it may at least help them not to make the same mistakes. However, by the time a couple have decided on divorce, it is probably too late, and there is an urgent need for readily available support services. Relate offers this, but its waiting lists are too long always to offer immediate help, and it has suffered from a restricted grant from central government.

The Church and divorce

The response of the Church to divorce is mixed. There is agreement that marriage ought to be for life, and that there should be the intention of permanence; but churches vary in whether they are willing to see divorcees remarried in church. The Catholic Church still maintains its opposition to divorce and remarriage, but other denominations are generally less rigid. The Greek Orthodox Church allows divorce, and in both the Church of England and in the Free Churches, such remarriages are largely left to the discretion of individual clergy. Some stress a rigorous approach, which identifies moral failings and calls for the Church to take a firm moral stand against cohabitation and divorce. Cohabiting couples, for example, are asked to live apart before their wedding, and/or make a public statement of repentance during the service. The children of cohabiting parents are refused baptism.[28] And Andrew Cornes, summarizing his book *Divorce and Remarriage*, writes that since Jesus teaches that marriage is an indissoluble bond, divorce simply is not possible. Divorcees who wish to remarry may find that hard to accept and turn away from the Church, but 'nothing less than this kind of explanation does justice to Christ's teaching and we are called to bear witness to his truth, whatever reception it and we are given.' It is possible to pray for a couple in a second marriage, since they have formed a new covenant, even if they should not have done so. However, Cornes argues that the Church should not give its seal of approval. Church members who divorce for unbiblical reasons, or remarry despite having Christ's teaching explained, should be subject to 'thoughtful disciplinary action' to lead them to repentance.[29]

There is an attractive simplicity in taking such an absolute line, and support can be drawn from the biblical tradition for it. Yet it is hard to reconcile that approach with Jesus' own pattern of ministry. He was more apt to denounce the religious leaders who took a legalistic or absolute line, than to condemn or exclude those who were doing wrong. Repentance for sin followed on from the encounter with Christ – it was not a precondition for being allowed into his presence. As Oppenheimer notes, 'If a serious attempt to apply his teaching leads straight into an unmerciful severity or a legalistic casuistry, we cannot have got it right.'[30] She gives a useful analysis of how Christ's teachings about divorce can be understood: neither taken as strict rules to be imposed, nor to be abandoned as too hard for anyone to keep. People are called to go beyond the law, into new understandings of love and faithfulness. Getting there, though, is the harvest of a whole way of life, never something which can be enforced. The emphasis for the Church must be on keeping alive the vision of what can be, whilst admitting that, for our 'hardness of heart', regulations which allow divorce and remarriage are needed. And whether or not a cohabiting couple or remarrying divorcees are deemed to be sinning, the aim should surely be to strengthen their relationship if it has a future, and to draw them nearer to God. This is a call frequently made by Dominian, who wants the Church to stop examining in detail where relationships contradict Christian tradition, and instead to use the opportunities to minister to people in relationships, raising their awareness of the God who is love. Concern for people in relationships is surely what should mark whatever the Church says on such subjects, rather than a condemnatory moral tone.

These themes of mercy and pastoral care inform Oppenheimer's discussion of the subject, though she insists that this must not mean letting go of the importance of marital vows. In order to safeguard the idea that marriage is characteristically indissoluble, and to provide the best conditions for marriages to flourish, divorce should be seen as a desperate necessity rather than an ordinary contingency. Losing a partner is rather like losing a hand, she says. It may be necessary, and we will get by if it happens, but it will still cause great hurt and distress, and amputation is a desperate remedy. If divorce has been necessary, however, the Church should welcome the chance to carry out remarriages. Our role is to celebrate with people, not to act defensively to ration God's grace. Anderson and Guernsey suggest that while we should not 'put asunder' what God has joined together, 'where God puts asunder as a judgement against sin and disorder . . . let not man uphold a law against God'. In a situation 'where sinful humanity has experienced brokenness and loss, the commandment of God is the presence of God himself at the center of that person's life to effect new being and new possibilities'. God is there to release from bondage and make all things new. However we ultimately express the theology of marriage, we have to include within it the knowledge that God is capable of bringing new possibilities out of brokenness:

> God is faithful to weak and problem-plagued marriages – not merely angry at unfaithfulness. God is patient and loving to marriages where love has been lost – not merely angry at our own anger and lovelessness. God is hopeful toward marriages that are ready to crash – not merely angry at our incompetence. God never gives up on his 'joining together,' because God is himself the covenant partner of marriage.[31]

Oppenheimer struggles after some way of recognizing that old obligations matter, and hints that the Church might devise some way of recognizing the ending of a previous marriage before people go on to remarry and to take on their new obligations before God. Thus remarriages are seen not as a matter of course, but as a special dispensation. Certainly some churches have devised liturgies to mark the ending of a marriage and this might be helpful for some people.

The values which sustain marriage include loyalty and faithful commitment, truthfulness and integrity, respect for the other person, and a proper appreciation of one's own needs. Is it a coincidence that, apart from the last one, these values are precisely those which get little public attention in society? The picture once again is of people with high ideals and positive human longings, in need of an infrastructure to support their relationships and allow them to flourish. A Church which concentrates on condemning offers little hope; compassion and clarity of vision are what is needed for the future.

Notes

1. C. Delphy and D. Leonard, *Familiar Exploitation* (Cambridge, Polity Press, 1992), p. 13.

2. M. Kolbenschlag, *Kiss Sleeping Beauty Good-bye* (San Francisco, Harper and Row, 1988 [1979]), p. 146.

3. H. Oppenheimer, *Marriage* (London, Mowbray, 1990), p. 5.

4. D. Dormer, *The Relationship Revolution* (London, One Plus One, 1992), p. 31.

5. K. Barth, quoted in R. Anderson and D. Guernsey, *On Being Family* (Michigan, William B. Eerdmans, 1985), p. 92. See also J. Dominian, *Passionate and Compassionate Love* (London, Darton, Longman & Todd, 1991), and G. Forster, *Marriage Before Marriage* (Nottingham, Grove Ethical Studies no. 69, 1988).

6. I have drawn on some points made by Dominian in an article in *The Tablet*, 4 July 1992, though I have expanded and added to them.

7. *Oxford Mail*, 19 November 1992. K. Kiernan and V. Estaugh found greater egalitarianism among cohabiting couples than among married ones. Their report *Cohabitation* (London, Family Policy Studies Centre, 1993) is a useful examination of cohabitation and social policy.

8. See, for example, the work of Talcott Parsons, or M. Young and P. Willmott, *The Symmetrical Family* (London, Routledge & Kegan Paul, 1973). Many Christian writers adopt this view in one form or another, as I showed in *A Woman's Work* (London, SPCK, 1989).

9. A. Phoenix, 'Mothers under Twenty', in A. Phoenix, A. Woollett, and E. Lloyd, eds, *Motherhood* (London, Sage, 1991).

10. Quoted in the *Guardian*, 17 August 1993.

11. Delphy and Leonard, *Familiar Exploitation*, p. 1. I am not systematically examining feminist analyses of the family in this book, but it is important to be aware of the points made, for they often act as a corrective to some of the idealized notions of family produced elsewhere. This is particularly true of white feminist writing. Feminists of colour may wish to affirm family more strongly because they experience it as a bastion against oppression. For example, see S. Thistlethwaite, *Sex, Race and God* (London, Geoffrey Chapman, 1990); and B. Bryan, S. Dadzie, and S. Scafe, *The Heart of the Race* (London, Virago, 1985).

12. J. Spong, *Living in Sin* (New York, HarperCollins, 1990).

13. J. Butterworth, 'Beauty and the Beast', *Family Life and Marriage Education Newsline*, Autumn 1991.

14. Oppenheimer, *Marriage*.

15. *Marriage and the Church's Task* (The Lichfield Report, CIO, 1978).

16. Dominian, *Passionate and Compassionate Love*, pp. 97 and 163.

17. Butterworth, 'Beauty and the Beast'.

18. D. Tannen, *You Just Don't Understand* (London, Virago, 1992).

19. House of Bishops, *Issues in Human Sexuality* (London, Church House Publishing, 1992).

20. Both Susan Dowell and Helen Oppenheimer have some useful points to make about the value of faithfulness in marriage.

21. *Family Policy Bulletin*, December 1991.

22. J. Dominian, *The Tablet*, 19/26 December 1992.

23. Dormer, *The Relationship Revolution*, p. 27.

24. *Economist*, 20 March 1993. I shall look at issues relating to one-parent families in the next chapter.

25. J. Conway, *Adult Children of Legal or Emotional Divorce* (Eastbourne, Monarch, 1991).

26. B. Tizard, 'Employed Mothers and the Care of Young Children', in Phoenix et al., eds, *Motherhood*, pp. 187ff.

27. There are a number of schemes which try to help married couples develop their relationship – for example, Marriage Encounter and Marriage Enrichment are well known. The Married Listening programme developed by the Family Caring Trust can be run at local level, and does not rely on both partners attending. Such programmes are no substitute for addressing external pressures on marriages, but can be helpful for some people. Simply knowing that others are or have been in similar situations can be useful.

28. An example of this line is Edward Pratt's booklet modelled on the Grove Ethical series, *Living in Sin?* (Southsea, St. Simon's Church, 1991).

29. *Church Times*, 2 April 1993. A. Cornes, *Divorce and Remarriage* (London, Hodder & Stoughton, 1993).

30. Oppenheimer, *Marriage*, p. 45.

31. Anderson and Guernsey, *On Being Family*, pp. 103-4.

chapter six

The Gender Agenda

*A way round most, if not all, of the emotional and psy-
chological ailments that so plague us as a society is to
have a stable family home with two parents who care for
one another and who live together in a close bond within
which the child feels securely loved.*

Andrew Stanway[1]

*A man within the bosom of his family, is often pilloried,
castigated and generally done over for his failures in
almost every aspect of caring, catering for and coralling
children. But, if he's 'no good' when he's present, why
do we also make an enormous fuss when he's not?*

Yvonne Roberts[2]

A key part of the 'family values agenda' is the insistence that two-
parent families are vital for the health of children and society. The
attack on one-parent families for producing delinquent children
and thus causing the breakdown of society suggests that two-
parent families ought to produce decent, properly behaved
citizens. Would that it were so! But there are plenty of delinquent
or damaged young people emerging from two-parent families, and
we cannot assume that keeping to one particular family form will
solve all problems. Reviewing the evidence, Utting et al. conclude
that family structure, for example being raised in a one-parent
family, is 'of less direct significance than the quality of care and

supervision that individual parents are able to provide'.[3] Stanway's claim, quoted above, has an element of truth in it, but goes too far. Good parenting by two parents can provide a secure psychological base, but there are many other factors with which children have to contend: relationships with friends and siblings, what happens to them at school, and external pressures from poor housing or poor health or tragedies in the family's life. My concern in this chapter is to look more precisely at why fathers and mothers are important, and at how presuppositions about gender affect what is happening in family life.

There is a widespread consensus that the ideal is for children to grow up with both father and mother. The 1990 European Values Study found that 84 per cent of people across Europe agreed with this statement – though this average conceals some diversity. Some 73 per cent of British people agreed, and interestingly in Sweden, where over half of all births are outside marriage, 82 per cent still thought children needed both father and mother. This is not the same thing as insisting that both parents are married or even live together, but it does suggest that both mothers and fathers will continue to be important for most people. This makes sense in terms of how most of us in Western culture see ourselves as drawing our identities from both our parents – though less importance may be attached to the biological father in some communities. But even where the influence has been negative, most of us find our parents contribute a great deal to our psychological identity. This is seen particularly in adopted children, who often have a deep need to know where they came from, which is quite separate from knowing the parents who have brought them up.[4] There are of course many cases where children do not know anything about their fathers, or know only their mother's view of him. Even just knowing that your father was there at conception and otherwise wanted nothing to do with you can have its influence on life, though I do not know to what extent there are problems associated with this.

The psychological link with biological parents is real enough, yet this is not generally given as a key reason why children need two parents. A number of arguments are used to support the two-parent family: some are based on a general idea that two is better than one; others assert that a mother and father bring something quite specific as female and male – apart from their obvious biological contributions.

Living in a one-parent family

We know that around one in five of all families with dependent children today are one-parent families – up from 8 per cent in 1971. Some 2 million children are affected. However, whether children brought up by a single parent are automatically worse off has been the subject of much debate (as I indicated in the previous chapter), for one-parent families are not a coherent group. Around 10 per cent are headed by fathers. Then there are young, never-married mothers and older mothers, often professional women, who have chosen to have a child alone. These two comprise 30 per cent of one-parent families, though the number of mothers in this category is increasing. The largest group are single mothers who are separated, divorced, or widowed, who form 60 per cent of one-parent families. There is also another group of mothers who are effectively single parents, because their husbands are absent much of the time – for example, in the forces, or in a job requiring extensive travel. Though I do not discuss them here, such families experience their own particular pressures. Commentators and politicians do not always differentiate, and it is not always clear whether they are talking about one-parent families, or the consequences of divorce on children. Yet there are some distinct differences, which affect the kind of support they need. It seems likely that divorce causes some psychological scars, which are more deep-rooted than those where one parent dies. However, children born to single parents in a community where this is the norm, are not affected by the loss of a parent in the same way. Making generalized statements about one-parent families increases the chance that social policy decisions will simply be irrelevant.

However, one factor which does link most one-parent families is their poverty. Children in one-parent families are 20 per cent worse off than those in two-parent households. Complaints about the single mothers who live on benefits tend to ignore the fact that benefit levels are quite low, and that it is not easy bringing up children in those circumstances. Many poor families do provide a caring upbringing for their children, but if they fail, their children have fewer alternative resources to draw on to offset the damage than those in affluent families. This is illustrated by the stories of people from different social groups in *Women's Ways of Knowing*.[5] The current attitude to single parents as morally suspect detracts attention from the fact that their circumstances make them and their children vulnerable. It is also much cheaper to call for a campaign against sin than to create housing and jobs. Critics like Norman Dennis – who argue that solving housing, employment, and poverty will not make a difference to the number of feckless single parents and absent fathers, because it is a moral problem – do have a point. Cultures and living patterns cannot be changed overnight. But creating better opportunities for those who are battered by circumstances is a step in the right direction.

Around half of divorced or separated mothers, and 90 per cent of single, never-married mothers, are on Income Support. This latter figure causes the government (and the public) great concern, and various policy options are being considered. Simply increasing welfare provision is too costly – and also fails to meet the needs of single parents, many of whom would like to be self-supporting if they could.[6] A difficulty here is that the desire to punish mothers who have babies outside marriage conflicts with the need to protect and support children, who are the innocent victims in it all. Reducing welfare provision might deter some young women from getting pregnant, but it might also lead to an increase in abortion, and threaten already vulnerable children's upbringing even further.

Some put forward the suggestion that young mothers and their children should be put in low-quality hostels, so as to deter others from getting pregnant in order to obtain housing. Yet the evidence that girls get pregnant simply to obtain housing tends to be fairly anecdotal, and at the time of writing evidence was being produced to suggest both that most teenage mothers live with their parents, and that young single mothers were not being more favourably treated for housing by local authorities than other families.[7] However, even if it was happening in large numbers, presumably the solution would be to make housing for single people more accessible, so they didn't need to do it. In fact, the reasons for teenage pregnancy seem to be more to do with a feeling that 'it won't happen to me', or the desire for emotional fulfilment which they think having a baby will bring – and which young men do not seem able to supply. Many teenage mothers lack self-esteem, and can find status and a sense of purpose in motherhood. This suggests the need to help girls to develop self-esteem, as well as to provide better information about contraception and the pressures of sexual relationships. More understanding about the hard realities of raising children might also help, though it is difficult when there are so many idealized images of mothers and babies.

Having sole responsibility for a baby when you are sixteen or eighteen can be enormously difficult, even in a council flat, and a child who spends its early years in a single dank room with a young inexperienced mother is getting a poor start in life. And unfortunately, babies have a habit of growing into children whose needs become much more complex as they grow older – something the romanticizing of the maternal instinct tends to obscure. Though some Christians are quick to pass moral judgements on such young women, the Church has a long history of helping young unmarried mothers, and still does a great deal. In recent years, the emphasis has been on helping them to take responsibility for their own and their babies' lives, by providing accommodation and personal support.[8]

The isolation of mother and baby is particularly acute in one-parent families, but it exists in two-parent families as well. Mothers without employment can spend upwards of ten hours a day alone with pre-school children, and the pressures are made worse if their housing is poor or the area they live in unsafe. Nevertheless, having a partner who can share even a small part of the burden makes a difference. There is something to be said for the argument that a two-parent family provides a chance of triangular relationships, offering different chances for negotiation, different possibilities. It is hard for one parent to be all things to all children, and when one is in a temper or ill it helps to have someone else to be there for the children. Because children too are different, it may be that one parent responds better to a particular child, or is good at relating to children of a particular age. One reason why I went on to have a second child was that I wanted to dilute my influence, and I'm grateful that the children have a father around for the same reason. As Chodorow puts it, 'children are better off in situations where love and relationship are not a scarce resource controlled and manipulated by one person only.' [9]

It may be much more difficult for single parents to get this kind of variety, unless they have other family members or close friends around them. It is not simply a matter of having different role models for children, of both sexes, but of them having other people to whom they belong, and to whom they can turn when the relationship with their one parent has gone wrong – a 'significant other'. However, a nuclear family may well still be too narrow for these purposes, and it can be of great benefit to children to have outside relatives or adult friends who can be turned to. A god-parent sometimes fulfils this function. The relationship between parent and child can be too close in a one-parent family, and not leave the child sufficient room to be themselves. Again, this is much less likely where the parent has a good network of other relationships, and the problem can easily happen in two-parent families as well, particularly where the marriage relationship is not good. A network of relationships is important too, in order to give a child a range of models of good parenting which they can draw on if they themselves become parents, especially if they do not find this at home.

It seems to be important for children's mental health that a distinction is made between the parental role, and the way a parent relates to other adults. Minuchin describes different units within families, which fulfil these different purposes. In the spousal unit, an adult couple respect, support, and nurture one another. They are each other's primary social partner, lovers, share significant interests, and so on. A single parent would look to have these needs met in a variety of ways. In fact, adult relationships will rarely meet all these expectations, but the key thing for Minuchin is that adults do not look to children to be their emotional caretakers. The parental task is distinct from this. Functional parents provide the basic necessities of life, are physically affec-tionate to children, establish clear rules and guidelines, respect and encourage each child's uniqueness, encourage their children's independence, and, in two-parent households, support each other's authority. For Minuchin, there is little overlap between these roles, for the emphasis in marriage (or other adult relationships) is on mutuality, whereas parenting is 'one-way'.[10]

This is saying something important, although it is too clinical an account of family life. Parents and children can and do play together, and share good and bad experiences as friends. A parent and child can be drawn together by a mutual interest, and it can be affirming for a child to know that a parent wants to spend time in their company. The experience of having and raising children can be profoundly fulfilling, and a source of personal development for adults, and this is one of the main reasons they choose to become parents. The main point stands, however, that whilst parents can welcome the times when they receive as much as they give from their children, they must not depend on a child to meet their needs, or make their children feel responsible for parental happiness. How far this extends to the relationship between parents and adult children is another matter. Adult children are likely to feel a responsibility for ensuring elderly or frail parents are cared for, but there will be limits to how far they can be responsible for making their parents happy.

One of each sex?

The parental role as described above may well be easier if shared between two people rather than limited to one, but if these are the only considerations, they might equally well be carried out by a committed gay or lesbian couple, or by other adults who are prepared to take the task on. From time to time the question emerges into public debate as to whether gay or lesbian couples ought to be allowed to adopt or have artificial insemination. Opinion tends to be against this – in one survey, though respondents were in the main liberal on gay issues, only 17 per cent agreed that suitably qualified gay men or lesbians should be able to adopt children. Generally, of those who object, many will do so on the basis that homosexuality is unnatural and wrong. For others, it may be a reluctance to place children in unconventional families, because of the teasing or confusion which might ensue. One lesbian couple featured in a newspaper article gave a different, more positive, picture of life with the children they had fostered and adopted. As one of them observed, it is perhaps odd that while government ministers stress that 'the vast majority of children benefit from having two loving parents of opposite sexes', they are happy for older or handicapped children, or those who cannot be placed elsewhere, to go to lesbian or gay couples.[11] It may be that this reflects the sense that a child should be given the chance to grow up in a conventional family if possible. With the beginnings of legal action by people who feel they have been dealt with badly when as children they were fostered or adopted, it is likely that society will opt for the safest course.

It is the fact that a same-sex couple have a sexual relationship that goes against society's norms, which makes gay and lesbian parenting an issue. There is much less concern where there are other arrangements. In the past, it would not have been unusual to find an unmarried female relative keeping house for a widowed mother, for example, without anyone raising questions about the harm caused by the absence of a man about the house.

Family health, particularly for some Christian commentators and those on the political Right, depends on men and women being prepared to adopt prescribed roles. The emphasis here is less on the healing marital partners can offer one another, than on their duties once they become parents. Thus women who become mothers have to be prepared to place themselves last, putting career prospects or their own interests on hold in order to devote themselves to their family; fathers need extra commitment to their employment in order to support their family, and to be authority figures in relation to their children.

I indicated in the previous chapter that marriage can seem like an enemy of equality between the sexes, and this comes to the fore where there are children. There is a change of atmosphere between literature about marriage which concentrates on the partners' relationship, and that addressed to parents. There can be reference to the duty to hang on when things are rough, but it is in the parental role that the sombre note of duty is sounded most strongly. It should be clear that where marriage is put forward in romantic terms, the responsibilities of children are going to come as a rude shock. It is no surprise that rather than holding marriages together, children can cause a marriage to fall apart.

Interestingly, there have been some recent comments that marriage and fatherhood are necessary in order to turn men into civilized citizens. This has been a theme in the past and, as Ehrenreich shows, the 1950s and 1960s saw many men rebelling against being trapped and domesticated by marriage.[12] Today Charles Murray berates single women who get pregnant for not doing their duty, which is to domesticate men: 'Young men are essentially barbarians for whom marriage . . . the act of taking responsibility for a wife and children, is an indispensable civilising force.'[13] One can see Murray's point, since marriage and fatherhood can mean a 'settling down'. Offenders may some-times be treated more leniently if they have got into a steady relationship, on the assumption that this can help them to reform – although there is some debate about whether this ought to happen. In fact, youthful marriages and early childbearing, especially alongside unemployment or low-paid employment, are all factors which predispose a marriage to break down, and there does not seem to be much that is positive in the relationship for the woman who has to do the civilizing. The theory is that she gets financial support, though men are less likely to be able to provide this reliably. The father's financial contribution to family life is getting a lot of attention at the moment. Absent fathers are expected to pay for the children they father, though not necessarily to father the children they pay for. It can be quite difficult for men to keep a close relationship with their children after divorce.

It is sometimes suggested that it is the failure to adhere to traditional roles which leads to marriage breakdown, although it is equally possible to answer that it is the restrictiveness of these roles which is the problem. Ehrenreich suggests that feminism and women's increasing refusal to put up with unsatisfactory marriages came after men had opted out of family life, and was not the cause of it. Much mainstream Christian theology, both in the past and today, adopts the notion of complementarity between men and women, and asserts that they bring specific qualities to their parenting. However, as I have shown elsewhere,[14] it is very difficult to pin down characteristics to one sex only. As women have shown they can do more and more in the world, and as men have felt more able to express their feelings, it has become apparent that femininity and masculinity are not so easily categorized.

Popular Christian literature about family life is often strong in asserting the need for 'traditional' male and female roles if the breakdown of society is to be prevented. Anne Ortlund's recipe for successful family life includes the necessity to 'recoup male and female roles'. Ortlund is willing for men and women to do non-traditional things, but only as long as the male is clearly the head, and the female respects him. Indeed, once a wife respects her husband properly, and the man's clout is acknowledged, the problems society has with lack of respect, crime, delinquency, and so on will be solved. The father's role is to affirm the maleness of boys by 'teaching them manners, respect for women and girls, and care and defense [sic] of them at all costs'. And 'God's normal way is for a man to command his children.'[15]

Men are often said to have a particular authority role in relation to women and children. This is true in much Catholic teaching as well as being a mark of much evangelical thought. A lot of evangelicals today speak of flexibility in male and female roles, yet find it hard to jettison completely the biblical idea of male 'headship'. There is a tendency to rewrite the notion of headship so that it has little practical significance. Moynagh, for example, says that the Bible does not see husbands as being in authority, but as bringing out the best in their wives. Scripture does not give rigidly prescribed roles for male and female, father or mother, says Moynagh. Husband and wife are to work as a team, assigning and adopting roles in whatever way is best for them. However, this is rather a forcing of the biblical text, since husbands in biblical societies were naturally thought to have authority over their wives.

Interestingly, Moynagh suggests that the first family relationship in Eden was that between Adam and his Father, and the Father/sonship relation will be central in paradise heaven too: 'Singleness will be universal in his family, and the key relationship will be between the Father and his children.'[16] Anthropological evidence suggests that the original bond is that between mother and child, not male and female; and the difference in gender from Moynagh's point is highly significant. There is much Christian writing which affirms the value of the mother-child bond. But we do not take that bond as the basic unit of human society, and explore what that might mean theologically – though it would be interesting to do so.

What is the point of fathers?

Fathers are given a unique role in the family, as head and authority figures. But what else are they supposed to bring? 'Fathering' generally means impregnating, rather than referring to the range of things fathers might do, yet there are beginning to be indications of just why fathers matter. There does seem to be a link between how we form our sexual identity and the way both our same-sex and other-sex parents behave. Spock, writing in his later years, observes that sexual identity is not about who does what, but about a sense of being female or male, which children get 'primarily from a satisfactory identification with the parents of the same sex, as well as from their glands and the shape of their bodies'.[17] This may mean adopting rather restrictive ideas of masculinity or femininity, if that is how their parents see them-selves.

One of the points made by A. H. Halsey in defence of the nuclear family is that children need the example of constant re-negotiations between mother and father if they are to form a view of women as anything other than objects of sexual manipulation and gratification.[18] In fact, because of the inequalities between women and men, children are more likely to learn about men's power over women than to discover that both are equal. There will be constant messages in who makes important decisions, who is responsible for family maintenance and so on, even in families where parents try to be fair with each other. Whether men model the polite protectiveness due to the weaker sex or are dismissive of 'Women!', it does not prepare boys to live alongside women as equals. In other families, the message is precisely that women can be abused verbally or physically, that men have a right to leisure and an independent social life which women do not. Some children would get a more positive picture of relations between the sexes by living with a mother on her own who relates well to men in general – and who is not enraged by an ex-partner.

Because fathers' role in families is more marginal and confused, there seems to be a particular problem here for boys. Thus Ingham concludes from her interviews with men that boys who lack a real model of maleness may develop stereotypical ideas: 'because of their hunger and unfulfilled need for an image of maleness', she says, 'boys are much more susceptible than girls to the negative effects of sex-role conditioning . . . boys are much more likely to conform to the socially acceptable image of what it means to be a man in order to complete their own sense of gender identity'.[19] It might help if society was clearer about why fathers were important, so that this became part of the male image; but such a change of attitude will take a long time, and the increasing number of young single women having babies, and not wanting involvement from the father, works against it. However, some signs of hope can be seen in the work beginning to be done with young men about fatherhood, which gives them a positive picture of the role they can play.[20]

Lee is sympathetic to the problems of boys, who are, she says, abandoned to their adolescence physically and emotionally. Boys may appear surly or uninterested, but actually may be very anxious about what is happening to them, and confused about the feelings of jealousy, vulnerability, fear, need, or aggression they experience. Lee suggests that 'Boys need fathers who will be to them what mothers generally are to teenage girls, able to identify with their often difficult and bewildering development as emotional and sexual beings.'[21] Yet fathers are unlikely to be able to provide this, unskilled as they are in talking about personal matters, and in a culture which still expects males to be tough and to know instinctively what sexual relationships are about. It is hard enough for many men to be emotionally articulate with their partners, and it may be even more difficult for them to deal with children who themselves may not be able to articulate feelings – though an articulate child may help a father to talk about feelings, by assuming it's natural to do so. Belenky et al. note how fathers often rely on mothers as intermediaries between them and their children, explaining to each how the other feels. One reason why fathers find it hard to maintain relationships with children after divorce may be that the father is then facing the children without an intermediary.

It is not simply a question of whether there is a father (or other close male figure) available, but what kind of man he is. The father or man close to children also needs to be caring, if boys are not to grow up violent, says Miedzian. A boy who can identify from the earliest age with a loving father has no need to repress the positive qualities of his own masculinity. Some people have made a link between violence and social deviance in boys and the lack of a proper father figure. There is something in this, though it is certainly not as simple as saying that boys in one-parent families are at risk, and those in two-parent families are not, since the former may have a caring grandfather, and the latter a deviant father.

Fathers are also influential in the development of their daughters' lives, affecting the way girls will form relationships with men later in life. Successful women often refer to the way their fathers encouraged them as a factor in their achievements, although this is less the case for younger women than for older ones. Equally, of course, abusive or unaffectionate fathers can cast long destructive shadows over the lives of both daughters and sons. Whilst we cannot define with any certainty exactly what fathers contribute, it is clear that they matter. Once a man has become a father, he must inevitably have an impact on his child's life – whether he takes no interest at all, is deliberately hurtful, or is consciously nurturing. It has long been clear that mothers have this kind of impact, but perhaps we have not always realized the extent to which it is true for men. Yet increasing evidence is emerging that an emotionally or physically absent father hurts his children, and perhaps especially leaves his sons floundering. Angela Phillips notes how men can feel trapped by the responsibilities of becoming a father, with no clear idea of what this ought to mean. Some are able to discover a positive meaning in fatherhood; others run away either physically or emotionally. Phillips concludes that:

> Men matter to their children not because of the genetic in-
> formation they impart or the money in the bank – they matter
> because of their contribution to their children's emotional
> growth. A father who is present in body but emotionally
> distant, violent, or abusive to the mother, provides a con-
> tribution far more negative than a father who is absent.

Mothers want more from men, not only for themselves but for their children, too. If there is a malaise at the heart of society it lies in the fact that too many men are taking too long to learn that the world has changed.[22]

There is something in this, and if fathers' main contribution is to children's emotional growth, clearly many are ill-equipped for such a role. This is not to say that it is all men's fault. It does take time to adjust to a changing world, and masculine ideologies constrain the options open for boys learning to be men. Yvonne Roberts points out that things are not always easy for fathers trying to do things differently. She concludes that though

> some fathers, driven by their own insecurity and licensed by society's traditions, do continue [to] exercise a primitive control through fear; they do abuse, batter, mentally destroy – and they do so on a significant scale because some still consider that this is part of a 'good' masculine upbringing. . . . other men, either by force of circumstance or volition, *are* trying to create new patterns of fathering. It may not be, as yet, an earth shaking trend, but it deserve[s] at least to be acknowledged and supported.[23]

Women themselves may make it harder for men to adapt, since to allow fathers a more powerful role in childrearing is to give up an area of women's traditional influence and expertise. But some way must be found of encouraging men to see the importance of fatherhood.

What is the point of mothers?

If fatherhood is problematic, at least we know what motherhood means – or at least we ought to if the sheer volume of works devoted to the subject is anything to go by. The trouble is that so much that is written either idealizes women as mothers, or treats motherhood as pathological. Mothers can cause havoc in children's lives, or can be spoken of as the civilizing influence that preserves society. Feminist analysis in recent years has been helpful in looking at the reality of what motherhood means for women, and allowing them to be seen as ordinarily flawed human beings.[24] Some 96 per cent of children live with their natural mother, and most of us have deep-rooted bonds with our mothers – even if in some cases these are based on hate rather than love. Most children also look to their mothers for emotional warmth and nurturing, as well as physical care, so that these elements are usually said to be characteristic of what mothers do. In fact, there are many different ways of mothering, and fathers can and do provide it in some circumstances, as can other relatives or adults.

Of particular interest in the context of this chapter is the social construction and valuation of motherhood. Much is made of the maternal instinct which propels women into motherhood, and makes them the best person to bring up their children; although at the same time severe moral judgements are made on young single mothers, whose behaviour is explained by greed for money or housing. Single mothers are thought not to have any of the instincts which will make them good parents, but instead are expected to raise children who will be delinquent. Similar moralizing occurs about mothers who have large families (especially if they are from minority ethnic communities) or mothers considered to be too old – there is periodic concern about post-menopausal women being allowed to conceive via medical intervention. There may be other grounds for arguing against teenage or granny-age pregnancies, but it should not be a surprise that many such women want to follow an 'instinct' which women are often told is basic to their nature.

It needs to be said that motherhood is experienced differently by women at different times and in different circumstances. Ethnicity, class, and time of life will all affect the way a woman sees herself in relation to her children. But what will be central, if she is to be an adequate mother, is that her children matter to her and that they know it. As I shall go on to argue, irritation and anger in family life are not entirely to be repressed, for they are signs of mattering. And though there is no universal model for mothering (or parenting in general), at the heart of what children need in addition to physical care is a loving, warm, reliable relationship. Women who have not themselves experienced this as children will find it very hard to reproduce it in their own families, though caring support at the right time can help them to develop the skills and confidence they need.

One element which is rarely associated with motherhood, but which may be important, is the need for respect. As I have said, it is fathers who are supposed to be authority figures, and the idea of respect for the father's authority is fundamental to many Christians' understanding of family values. But the lack of respect for mothers as people in their own right, with their own needs and interests, perpetuates problems in families and society. Where women's needs are systematically denied, they fail to be all that they could be, and children fail to learn that they must taper their needs to those of others, and to take some responsibility for themselves. In a society where women's authority is exceptional, it becomes difficult – particularly for mothers parenting alone – to exercise appropriate control. We tend to allocate values of authority and caring to fathers and mothers respectively, with the idea that the two-parent family will thus provide the complete range. The problem is not only that men and women do not fit those categories exactly, but that we deny an important part of their humanity if we fail to recognize men's caring and women's authority – and I shall return to this point later.

The ideal put forward by many people is of shared parenting, rather than allocating roles. Some feminists like Chodorow have argued that the fact that we are parented by a woman is responsible for hostility towards female power in general. The ideal of shared parenting features heavily in many childcare manuals and magazines, and the symbol of the New Man complete with baby was a common one towards the end of the 1980s and in the early 1990s. Unfortunately, reality has not kept pace with the image; though there are changes, fathers in general are still far from being equal to women in the time and energy they give to their children.

Some have sought to discover a model for human parenting by looking at Jesus' human parents. Mary may be seen as the ideal mother, although this usually involves projecting onto her a particular view of what mothers ought to be like. Some will stress her submissiveness and self-sacrifice, and others her independent spirit. Similarly, some theorize that Joseph must have been a particular kind of father for Jesus to have grown up as he did, either strict or nurturing, depending on one's perspective. Rather than believing Jesus must have had an ideal mother or father, it is more likely that he had 'good enough' parents. His development was not hindered by extremes of circumstance or parental behaviour. All we can say is that he must have had enough love and care to enable him to be fully the son of God, and that misunderstandings and disagreements with his parents were no barrier to this.

Christianity has a particular interest in fatherhood, having used it as the prime metaphor for the Godhead throughout its history. How far either our understanding of human fatherhood, or our understanding of God have developed as a result, is a hard question to answer. The idea of God as Father has not been universally helpful, and should not be seen as the only way we should speak of God. Those whose experience of fathers has been destructive may associate all sorts of negative values with God's fatherhood. Thistlethwaite notes that in the black community (in the United States at least) there has been much less interest in God as Father than in the image of Jesus as the Lord, who is alongside in times of trouble. Perhaps there can be no single right model of God's relation to and creation of the world and its inhabitants. There is both the sense of achievement, the potter moulding the clay, the creator spreading out the skies, and the more intimate sense of a mother who says of her newborn: 'this is my body, this is my blood'.

Unfortunately for human parenting, the predominant image of God the Father is of a stern and distant authority figure. Roger Scruton, for example, in his essay in *Fatherhood*,[25] speaks of God as Father as a distant figure, creating something separate from himself, who cannot be represented by soft and intimate female imagery. Such descriptions tell us more about the writers' perceptions of their parents than about God. Moynagh gives a rather strange exposition of the relation between God as Father and Jesus as Son in a search to find a lesson for us: 'At the cross . . . Father and Son experienced some of the central hurts of family life.' For the Son felt abandoned by the Father, and the Father faced having a rebellious son. I can imagine that the idea of God identifying with the sufferings of family life might provide comfort to Christians, but it stretches the Father/Son language of the New Testament too far. 'Christian parenting ought to display the same characteristics as the Father's parenting of the Son', says Moynagh,[26] but given that the discipline experienced by the Son is identified with death on the cross, it is perhaps a little harsh. McCloughry too asserts that 'God's character and relationship with Jesus Christ is normative for [men's] fathering.'[27] I am sympathetic to the attempt to give men good models for fatherhood, but we cannot reduce the relations of the Trinity to the provision of purely masculine role models. What we can know is that what is good about human parenting is a reflection of what is good in God, and can be modelled on God's love for us – though neither mothering nor fathering alone tells us all there is to know.

Notes

1. A. Stanway, Preparing for Life (London, Viking, 1988), p. 12.

2. Y. Roberts, *Mad About Women* (London, Virago, 1992), p. 90.

3. D. Utting, J. Bright, and C. Henricson, *Crime and the Family* (London, Family Policy Studies Centre, 1993), p. 20.

4. I do not know whether there are any similar feelings among children conceived by AID (Artificial Insemination by Donor) or by self-insemination. The law has not recognized the need for a child to know its father in this area, as it has done in cases of adoption.

5. M. Belenky et al., *Women's Ways of Knowing* (New York, Basic Books, 1986), p. 160.

6. See *One-parent Families: Policy Options for the 1990's*, from the Joseph Rowntree Trust, for a useful discussion of the pros and cons of the different ideas put forward.

7. See, for example, the report published by the Institute of Housing in October 1993.

8. For example, in my own area, the Oxford Diocesan Council for Social Work has some seven hostels for young single mothers, and there is a similar picture in other Anglican dioceses, as well as work done by other denominations.

9. N. Chodorow, *The Reproduction of Mothering* (Berkeley, California, University of California Press, 1978), p. 217.

10. S. Minuchin, *Families and Family Therapy* (Cambridge, Massachusetts, Harvard University Press, 1974).

11. *Observer*, 25 October 1992.

12. B. Ehrenreich, *The Hearts of Men* (London, Pluto Press, 1983).

13. Quoted in Roberts, *Mad About Women*, p. 140.

14. A. Borrowdale, *Distorted Images* (London, SPCK, 1991). I also look in more detail at male and female roles in *A Woman's Work* (London, SPCK, 1989).

15. A. Ortlund, *Disciplines of the Home* (Milton Keynes, Word UK, 1990), pp. 69ff. James Dobson, widely read among evangelicals, holds a similar view.

16. M. Moynagh, *Home to Home* (London, Daybreak, 1990), p. 102.

17. B. Spock, *Parenting* (London, Michael Joseph, 1989), p. 57.

18. A. Halsey, *Guardian*, 26 February 1993.

19. M. Ingham, *Men* (London, Century, 1984), p. 113.

20. There is some reference to such work in Utting et al., *Crime and the Family*, and I have heard of a few other schemes, though these do not seem to be written up systematically as yet.

21. C. Lee, *Friday's Child* (Wellingborough, Thorsons, 1988), p. 57.

22. A. Phillips, *Independent*, 9 July 1993.

23. Roberts, *Mad About Women*, p. 119.

24. I looked at this at length in *A Woman's Work*.

25. R. Scruton, in S. French, ed., *Fatherhood* (London, Virago, 1992).

26. Moynagh, *Home to Home*, pp. 94 and 121.

27. R. McCloughry, *Men and Masculinity* (London, Hodder & Stoughton, 1992), pp. 162-3.

chapter seven

Not Saving,
but Frowning

Children won't do what they ought
If you beat them with a rod.
Children thrive, children grow
When taught by words, and not a blow.
Evil words, words unkind
Will do harm to a child's mind.

Walther von der Vogelweide c.1200[1]

Christian children all must be
Mild, obedient, good as he.

C.F. Alexander

Well, I haven't much to give them, poor things, so I give
them their own way.

Parent, 1882[2]

God was too far out all my life
Not saving but frowning.

After Stevie Smith[3]

Over the past few years I have read a great many books about
children and childrearing, from both Christian and secular
perspectives, and it has been depressing to note how many of the

secular books single out religious households as being particularly prone to damaging children emotionally and physically by their over-rigid stances and their emphasis on the hierarchical ordering of family life. At the same time, many of the Christian writers attack the secular 'experts' for having created a crisis in society through their over-permissive attitudes. Why is there such a gap between what many Christians perceive as God's way of bringing up children, and the view of so many psychologists? Is it that Christians are upholding God's biblical standard in the face of an immoral and ultimately destructive secular ideology? Or are we inflicting untold harm on children, in direct contravention of biblical teaching? This chapter begins my attempt to unravel some answers.

Some historical aspects

I have already shown that the thesis that society was properly ordered in the past is seriously flawed. Similarly, the idea that children were properly disciplined until the permissive liberals of the 1960s got to work, does not stand up to analysis. Though I can do no more here than refer briefly to historical attitudes towards childrearing, it is well worth studying them both for their own interest and as a way of putting the attitudes of our own day into context.[4] The attempt to show a clear progression from early brutality towards children to more enlightened attitudes today usually founders, since parents have generally been a mixture of the careless and the caring. Yet there does seem to have been a movement away from the idea of seeing children merely as the property of their parents towards the idea that they are individuals with their own rights.[5] Such a movement is linked to the growth of individualism in the West over the last couple of centuries, though it is also made more possible because families have progressively had fewer children and the mortality rate has dropped. Through all this, though, it is possible to detect a continuing tension between those who want to stress punitive discipline and those who want to take a more lenient approach: the authoritarian and the liberal positions.

Thus whilst some Puritans in the seventeenth century stressed that children were wayward from the cradle, and needed to have evil driven out of them, others saw infants as blank sheets of paper, needing more gentle guidance. Similar debates can be traced in the Victorian period. Again, we have the idea that children were treated strictly, expected to be seen and not heard; but in fact, as Hardyment shows, plenty of parents of that era saw things differently, and writers on childcare anticipated some of the best insights of child development today. Literature in the twentieth century shows how fashions swung between regimented and permissive approaches to rearing children. The work of John Watson was popular between the wars, for example. He wanted to eliminate emotion from treatment of the child, and follow completely scientific principles: 'There are rocks ahead for the over-kissed child.'[6] Parents did not necessarily follow these principles slavishly, but they did have an influence. Many mothers now in their sixties and seventies recall trying to follow the rigid schedules recommended by Truby King, albeit against their instincts.

Hardyment suggests that the greatest revolution in approaches to childrearing at the beginning of the twentieth century ·was the new concentration on the habits and wills of children, rather than their moral conscience. Much of what was said in the earliest writings about children took place in a Christian context, though there was little direct theological reflection on children as individuals. For example, De Mause argues that the opposition of the Church to infanticide was based more on the notion that it was bad for the parent's soul, than on the idea that it was bad for the child. But the idea behind childrearing was that moral conscience had to be developed, so that children would learn to serve others and be prepared to deny themselves when necessary. Modern manuals concentrate much more on what will best enable a child to flourish. There is often an underlying belief that children should develop into the sort of people who are sympathetic and co-operative in their work and play; but it has been difficult to find the moral language to express this, now that Christian language and tradition have lost their place.

We have come to rely on the idea that children will naturally tend to be kind and co-operative, and that if they aren't, their self-interest can be appealed to: 'If you steal, no one will want to be your friend.' 'But', said one nine-year-old, 'stealing's all right as

112

long as no one ever finds out something's been stolen.' A difficult one, this, for who has been hurt if the item is never missed? Perhaps the child can come to see that getting away with one theft may lead to others, but it also requires complex arguments about what happens to a society if people cannot trust one another, which may not make sense to a child who is talking only about their own action. It is much easier to be able to say that God forbids stealing, sees all we do, and perhaps also add that those who disobey God will be punished. No wonder government ministers urge that children should have the fear of hell put into them, for we have difficulty setting out moral precepts on their own. This is not to say that people lack morals, and, as Gill has shown, Christian precepts are embedded in society's value systems. However, it is hard to find the right language with which to teach morality. Theology, which at one time provided a *raison d'être* for childrearing, has not really developed new thinking for the changed climate. Indeed, it is noticeable how much of what Christians say on the subject takes no account of all the study of child development, but insists that the only suitable model stems from 2,000 years ago.

Childrearing precepts have always been influenced to some extent by what was going on in the world around, the stability of the social order, the intellectual debates of the day. In the twentieth century, two World Wars have left their mark, as have technology and increased affluence in society. Psychology has given new insights into how we become the people we are, and how we are damaged. There have been attempts to regulate the processes of giving birth and childrearing according to principles of scientific management. The state began to have much more to do with these things, through its welfare provision, and the medicalization of childbirth.

Though it is fifty years on, society is still living with the fallout from the Second World War, and the hopes and fears it inspired. Once the war had ended, notes Hardyment, 'Reaction from austerity, military discipline and sudden death made parents peculiarly inclined to indulge the new generation.'[7] As men came home from the war, and a domestic idyll took root, mothers were encouraged to think their proper place was in the home – an ideology that is still prevalent, though contradicted by practice.

Ehrenreich and English study the way permissiveness grew out of and affected the national mood in the United States. As the economy became increasingly dependent on individual consumption, experts managed to discover that self-indulgence was good for the individual personality as well as commercial prosperity. Children would develop naturally as long as they received unquestioning, spontaneous, warm, all-enfolding love.

There was some criticism of over-permissiveness by the early 1950s, a voice which became stronger as the 1950s and 1960s unfolded. The trouble was that American youth, and its males in particular, were causing problems – gang violence, failure to show strength of character in Korea, political protest over Vietnam, demonstrations on civil rights. Blaming Dr Spock and 'spoiled brats who never had a good spanking', as Agnew did, was far too simple – protesters came from both authoritarian and permissive backgrounds. And it enabled politicians to ignore the political implications of such unrest – a process which happens in Britain at times. It also helped to perpetuate the idea of youth as the enemy.[8] The idea that children could be entirely indulged lost favour. This was the era of titles like Dobson's *Dare to Discipline*, first published in 1970,[9] and it becomes easier to understand Dobson's preoccupations if we look at the background against which it first appeared. And yet, one of Dobson's solutions to a crisis in family life is for mothers to stay at home and make their families their top priority - something which was actually happening in the 1950s, and contributing to the problem. As Friedan notes: 'the mothers of the maladjusted soldiers, the insecure and impotent postwar males, were not independent educated career women, but self-sacrificing, dependent, martyred-housewife "moms"'.[10]

Permissive parenting

Permissiveness is one of three distinct modes of parenting which gets identified in literature about childrearing – though the names given to these modes sometimes differ.[11] This analysis tends to stereotype the different approaches, but I wish to use it for the moment. 'Permissive parenting' is usually represented as affirming children's natural impulses, not making demands for orderly behaviour, and avoiding any control. Children are allowed to express themselves, even if this means walking all over their parents and being as rude as they like to them. It may seem Christian, in its stress on kindness and long-suffering, although it is a limited view of love which ignores its hard demands. The theory is that children's autonomy should be respected, in order that they may grow into mature, balanced people. However, the impression given is of rather unpleasant, dictatorial little monsters, as with the children described by Steiner, who will 'refuse to go to bad schools, they will refuse to follow oppressive rules, they will demand to be heard when they speak, they will ask for everything that they want 100% of the time and demand that their wishes be considered on an equal footing with the grownups in the household'.[12] Though Steiner says later that parents should not let their children oppress them, one wonders how one gets the message across to children who so clearly know their rights to refuse or demand. Dobson is scathing about the application of such permissiveness in education, quoting the example of Summerhill – though I would query how widely these extremes of permissiveness were practised in the British educational system.

Notwithstanding the few writers Dobson notes, I have not myself come across any 'experts' who advocate letting children follow their wishes entirely. This may be a difference between the United States and Britain, although Dobson's ideas are adopted by many Christians in Britain as though the situations were parallel. It is true that some parents have picked up the idea that children should be indulged and not expected to obey, and it has been said that the problems of today's children are related to under-control, rather than over-control as in the past. This is a theme developed by Novak in *The Parent Trap*, where it is suggested that children brought up permissively go on to have no respect for any kind of authority. Says Novak:

> I spent my whole childhood being intimidated by the look in my father's eyes and I seem to have spent my whole adulthood being intimidated by the look in my children's eyes. Being told no is the point around which you define yourself: you either rebel or accept, but if there are no boundaries you are left to wander around the maze of your own feelings or this leads to a terrific loss of direction and loss of standards because you don't know what matters.[13]

Faced with a lack of any boundaries, children's behaviour may become worse and worse, in effect saying: 'How bad do I need to be before you'll control me?'

Yet few parents believe in total permissiveness as a philosophy. Indeed, those parents who do advocate it may expect to influence their children's behaviour through showing approval or disapproval, even if they take no other steps. Judgemental use of the label 'permissive parenting' fails to address the problem adequately. Most parents believe their children should be under control, but are uncertain as to how to achieve this. They are ineffective at control, not aiming to be permissive. This is perhaps borne out by the former teacher and inspector of inner-city primary schools who suggested to me that it was not that children's behaviour had got worse, but that our ability to manage them as parents and teachers had deteriorated. If children consistently take no notice of their parents' efforts at control, the parent may give up the attempt. Sometimes there are external factors which make children difficult to control, such as stress in the family, or hyperactivity in children. Also, parents' own attitudes can be influenced by the circumstances surrounding pregnancy and birth. Parents may be more inclined to indulge a child born after years of infertility, or who has been through a life-threatening illness, for example. 'Indulgence' may be a better way of describing the attitude of many parents, who wish to give their children the best they can, particularly of material goods. This may include indulging children's bad behaviour, but can also go alongside a belief in the need for control. It may, however, be true that some of the lack of parental confidence and effectiveness is the result of a misunderstanding of current childrearing ideas, and I shall return to this point later.

Those who are called 'permissive' may simply be 'advocating a more tolerant approach to children. Rather than seeing them as born 'bad' and in need of control, they are seen as born 'good'. The parental task is to allow the good to develop. As I have said, this idea has a long history, but many of those who have a 'permissive' tag still insist that limits need to be set if healthy development is to happen. This would be true of Spock and Penelope Leach, for example. Spock is popularly supposed to have gone back on his earlier commitment to permissiveness, having seen the havoc wrought by the so-called 'Spock-marked generation', though he denies the charge. Similarly, Leach has been criticized for letting babies dictate their mother's response – but although I have had my own arguments with her at 3 o'clock in the morning, when my baby wasn't doing what she said it should, Leach is clearly aware of the need to provide boundaries for children.

Bruno Bettelheim's work fits the 'permissive' category in terms of his attitude towards discipline and control. He suggests that, 'A parent who respects himself doesn't need to buttress his security by demanding respect from his child.' Such a parent,

> secure in himself, will not feel his authority threatened and will accept his child – at times – showing lack of respect for him, as particularly young children are occasionally apt to do. He knows that if it happens, it is due to immaturity of judgement, which time and experience will eventually correct. . . . a demand for respect reveals to the child an insecure parent who lacks the conviction that this will be given to him naturally.

The lack of self-confident parents can make the child grow into an insecure person.

Further, says Bettelheim, whilst 'criticism or fear of punishment may restrain us from doing wrong, it does not make us wish to do right. The only effective discipline is self-discipline.' And:

> It is not much of a conscience which tells us not to do wrong because we might be punished. The effective conscience motivates us to do right because we know that otherwise we will suffer all the pain and depression of feeling bad about ourselves. In the last analysis, we will reliably do right only in order to prevent the pangs of conscience – to feel good about ourselves, not to avoid punishment.[14]

Authoritarian parenting

This attitude is poles apart from the authoritarian parenting which is at the other end of the spectrum, and which demands obedience from children, and believes strongly in discipline. Here the parent, particularly the father, is modelled after a God who is 'not saving but frowning'. Martin Herbert speaks of parents who 'attempt to shape, control and judge the behaviour and attitudes of their children according to unbending standards of conduct, usually absolute standards, often determined by theological considerations'. They value obedience as a virtue, believe in indoctrinating a child with respect for authority, and for the preservation of the traditional order.[15] A good example of this approach is Anne Ortlund in *Disciplines of the Home*. For her, respect for leadership is the glue that holds society together, and the one from whose respect it springs is the wife in the home. As Ephesians 5.33 says, she is to respect her husband, because

> the wife who challenges, contradicts, doubts, overrides, and negates her husband will probably produce offspring who later challenge teachers, contradict government, doubt laws, override police, negate courts, and in general produce a hassled, ineffective, exhausted society. If father has no clout, eventually neither does anyone else.

However, she continues, if the wife respects her husband, the children respect their parents and all government authorities as well. The child who grows up under authority as well as love, learns to be patriotic and to fight for his country; to obey governments even if they are bad, to pay taxes, and not to speak against government leaders.[16]

Discipline is the essential thing, Ortlund believes, and begins with parents: 'As you submit to the discipline of your heavenly Parent, you have every right to expect that your own children will submit to yours.' Toddlers are to be taught to memorize the scripture `children obey your parents'. And if they disobey, then 'sin and pain must early be linked together in their minds' – from two upwards, 'an ignored "no" should be followed by a short quick spanking. When they knowingly, wilfully sin, then there must be pain. . . . Punishing is the deliberate infliction of hurt. . . . it's crucially important that children grow up convinced that sin and hurt go together. That's how they learn to fear and hate sin.'[17]

Ortlund is keen to point out that this should not lead to abuse, but unfortunately it can easily do so. Margaret Kennedy, in an article entitled 'Christianity - Help or Hindrance for the Abused Child or Adult?', writes that 'in many fundamentalist religions, the power role of the parents, the Old Testament beliefs in punishment for sin, and the fear of a constantly tempting world are dynamics that make many parents tragically overreact in the discipline and punishment of their children. The need to "drive out the devil" is many times the justification given by religious, neurotic, overly punishing, assaultive parents.' She further notes the link between sexual abuse and an overly moralistic style of parenting, quoting a clinical psychologist who says, 'Despite the clear prohibition of incest in Leviticus 6.18, the majority of reported aggressors are regular church attenders. . . . the adult males tend to be very devout, moralistic and conservative in their religious beliefs.'[18]

Though a few may find the strength to rebel, most children brought up under a strict authoritarian regime tend to be conforming, unimaginative, biddable, and lacking self-reliance. Such qualities can of course be useful ones to encourage for those in power, and Ortlund is quite explicit about this. There is some evidence that, in the past at least, those in the lower social classes were more likely to use highly authoritarian and non-verbal means of control, with threats and physical punishment. The middle classes are more likely to use verbal, democratic reasoning, and this helps to equip their children to use the system. Working-class children have been expected to conform and accept their place, and the first schools for working-class children were originally designed to give them standards of obedience, punctuality, cleanliness, and deference to authority.

'Respectful' parenting

Having described these two extremes, the natural solution is to introduce a third idea, of parenting that sets limits, but is also kind, understanding, and so on. Here, parents are expected to listen to their children, and involve them in decision-making when appropriate, but the parents are ultimately in charge. They will expect obedience at times, but will give reasons for it. One example of this might be the McGinnises's book *Parenting for*

Peace and Justice, and its sequel, which looks at how things have developed ten years on. They argue for a style of parenting which they call mutual, as opposed to being permissive or authoritarian: 'Parents do not make all the decisions; but neither do they give in to the children when their own essential needs, values, interests, and responsibilities are at stake.'[19] 'Mutual' may not be the best word, given that children do not have the same responsibilities towards their parents, nor the same power. A number of other people use the term 'authoritative parenting', which I suspect is more to do with the convenience of the word paralleling 'authoritarian' than with the suitability of what it actually means. I wonder whether we could speak of 'respectful' parenting. Though the word can be used to indicate submissiveness, which is certainly not the point here, it does convey the idea that parents should respect their children and be civil to them; and in a relationship full of respect, the children should also learn to respect their parents. (I shall unpack this idea at greater length in the course of the next chapter.)

Generally speaking, the advice offered to parents, over the last ten years at least, falls into this category, and there is some evidence that this style is the most helpful if we wish to develop responsible, thinking adults. Spock discusses some experiments on forms of leadership, and relates the outcome to the way parents ought to behave. In one instance, a group of boys were set a task, and given a highly authoritarian leader. Whilst the leader was present, the task was addressed well, but when the leader was absent, the boys just messed about, and took out their resentment on each other or the work. When the boys were given a leader with a very *laissez-faire* style, the boys just fooled around. Some made an effort to get things going, but found it impossible. With a democratic leadership, where the leader controlled and guided, but made space for the boys to be involved, they carried on with the task when he wasn't there.[20] It could be argued that this is more the type of leadership that Jesus exercized, which was designed to inspire his followers to carry on with his work once he was no longer physically present. Yet he left his Spirit with them, and did not entirely abandon them. The authoritarian style of leadership is suitable for some tasks, but not for teaching co-operation and responsibility. As Virginia Satir comments: 'It is beyond me how judgement can be taught through "obey me" techniques, and if there is any one thing we need in this world, it is people with judgement.'[21]

However, this description of two extremes and a better, middle way has its problems. Many writers on childcare resist being put into a clear-cut category. James Dobson, for example, would be placed by many of his critics under the authoritarian label, but much of what he says falls into the middle band of firm parenting accompanied by a lot of love and gentle understanding. His stress on the need for physical punishment seems to fit clearly into the authoritarian mode, though he sets quite a number of caveats around it, so that it is actually quite a small element of a parent's repertoire. Again, whilst I disagree with Ortlund at many points, she also has some very sensible things to say about parenting – for example, on slowing down and listening to children. Similarly, a writer like Andrew Stanway might seem to belong in the permissive mode. He makes the baby's or child's needs and wishes central in a way that feels exhausting just reading it! Babies are to be carried around with the mother all day, share the parental bed, and mothers shouldn't have jobs, or very much life of their own either. Yet again, this is an unfair representation of Stanway's stance as a whole, for he also stresses the need to provide limits, and describes himself as recommending authoritative parenting.

Underlying convictions

What makes the difference is not so much what is actually said about the practicalities of parenting, but the underlying philosophy and theology of the writers. Thus the McGinnises and Dobson have a lot of agreement on strategy when it comes to dealing with children, but seem poles apart because they start at profoundly different points, politically and theologically. The McGinnises are politically on the Left, committed to social justice, feminism, anti-racism, and so on. Dobson and Ortlund have a stance overtly associated with the political Right: both blame feminism for social and family ills. Ortlund's agenda is that of the Right-wing moral majority in the United States, with its emphasis on respecting authority in the form of the flag, God, and government. In

Britain, it is Conservatives who are most likely to use the language of discipline and moral values, although some Labour politicians have begun to speak in this way as well.

The whole thesis behind Ortlund's writing, for example, is that 'this world's culture is an avalanche sliding towards hell . . . and you don't want your own precious children to go with it'.[22] Parents must therefore take drastic steps. For some who share this view, children are born with an inbuilt propensity towards sin, which needs to be removed through baptism and/or strict discipline. The idea that, at baptism, newborn babies are said to have passed from darkness to light reflects a belief in innate neo-natal sinfulness.

Such a view has a long history in Christian tradition, of course, and it has led to ill-treatment of children, when parents try to beat the devil out of them. It may also be reflected in the readiness of many parents to speak of babies as being naughty when they cry or refuse food – and sometimes to use physical punishment to 'teach them a lesson'. Dobson's followers quote Psalm 58 to show that human beings 'go astray as soon as they are born, speaking lies'. Even babies can 'tell lies' by crying in anger.[23] Feeding on demand and picking up a baby whenever it cries are said to encourage sinful selfishness in the infant. Many writers suggest that babies respond to some regularity, but the key difference here is whether this is seen as being about the baby's physical needs, or a battle for its soul.

Ortlund's own picture is of children who are essentially unformed and pliable – *Children Are Wet Cement* is the title of one of her books, and similar images are also found in Christian tradition – and, therefore, need to be moulded to the right shape. If the godly parent doesn't do this, the secular and evil world will. The emphasis must therefore be as much on protecting children from outside pressures as teaching them good Christian values. Those who take this line therefore place a lot of emphasis on regulating television, pop music, and so on. There is no room here for a theology of creation and incarnation: only within the Christian community can goodness and God survive.

Born bad or naturally good?

The idea that some babies are born bad is resurrected in many discussions of crime. We get references to some children being born as 'thoroughly nasty pieces of work'. There is even talk of a 'gene' for violent, antisocial behaviour. Yet, as I have already pointed out, the most that can be said is that some people will be more prone to reacting to hostile environmental conditions with aggression and violence. As one commentator put it on a television documentary examining the roots of violence, 'if we want to make a child violent, we do not start with biology, we bring him up in a harsh, rejecting home'.[24] Michael Ignatieff wrestled with the thought that social circumstances create violence, when he reflected on atrocities in Bosnia, and commented that the 'idea that some men are innately evil seems to evade the real difficulty, which is to explain how perfectly ordinary fathers and husbands can be slowly degraded, by the dull impulsion of carnage, into the sort of person who torches a basement with women and children inside it'.[25] This example reminds us that human beings can behave atrociously, particularly when they act as groups. I have not looked at this aspect of human behaviour in this book, but the relation of individual wickedness to the actions of groups and nations is important.

The philosophy behind the work of people like Bettelheim is that children are fundamentally inclined to be good, and the duty of the parent is to provide an atmosphere in which this can flourish, which means avoiding too much criticism and restrictive control. Children need limits, but are to be respected as individuals with their own rights and feelings. Winnicott, for example, speaks of the innate goodness of the baby, its innate capacity to love. Proper management will allow a baby to develop a co-operative attitude. Destructive impulses, for Winnicott, are a response to frustration, rather than being bad; and he criticizes the idea of 'original sin'. His view is that 'to treat a child as a being "conceived and born in sin" and thereby as one who must be taught about goodness as though it were something foreign to his nature, is to ignore the incipient moral goodness with which the child is endowed'.[26] Theologically, children can be regarded as being made in the image of God, with a core of generosity and compassion, and a readiness to love others, which can be developed under the right circumstances. In both developmental and theological terms, it makes no sense to speak of babies and small children as capable of being sinful – that is, deliberately doing wrong. For those who share this perspective, though there are dangers in the world, children's ability to trust others and enjoy the world must not be destroyed. In Christian terms, this can be linked to a belief that God created the world with its people, and saw that it was good. It offers hope that whatever sin means in its structural and individual manifestations, the world contains much that is good, and what is wrong is redeemable.

The potential for evil and goodness

The paradox is that God is both everywhere within the world, yet sin continues to be woven into the structures and the hearts of individuals. What many psychologists and theologians today hold is that human beings are born with the capacity both for good and evil. Muriel Frampton makes an interesting comparison between Winnicott's view and that of Reinhold Niebuhr. Niebuhr's position, which sees the world as created essentially good by God, but blighted by the inevitability of human sin, suggests that 'even with Winnicott's "facilitating environment" enabling children to grow up into stable adults with a healthy moral sense, society would still reveal the negative side of man's nature'.[27] Interestingly, Spock suggests that 'religious and ethical ideals should be balanced by discussion of how natural it is for human beings to be greedy, selfish, procrastinating, lazy, irritable, angry, jealous and impelled by sex, so that individual children won't get the idea that only they are naughty'. We must avoid teaching them that humans are predominantly bad and only God is good, for 'the positive drives in people – love, generosity, cooperation, loyalty and the drive to nurture – are stronger than the negative drives, provided that individuals have had the benefit of growing up in a loving family'.[28] Destructive impulses are not alien or demonic, but part of who we are, for which we must take responsibility.

Rosalind Coward discusses this in an article taking issue with the way public opinion oscillates between demonizing and over-sentimentalizing children. If we think a child is naturally unaggressive, and without sexuality, then when they behave in aggressive ways or reveal their sexuality at a young age, blaming evil is the only solution. But whether we are naturally loving or difficult people, all of us are born with both destructive and constructive capacities, and 'With good parenting or education, the constructive elements of the personality are supported and gradually gain the upper hand.'[29] The behaviour of the most difficult children is easily categorized as evil, but as Yapp shows, "problem children" behave as they do because they have the feeling that not enough is being done to ensure their survival. Their behaviour has a kind of logic to it, however disruptive it is: 'They may show insecure behaviour: "I can't survive in this world"; behaviour against their own interests (even suicide): "I don't deserve to survive"; developmentally stuck behaviour: "I don't want to take responsibility for my survival"; aggressive behaviour: "I have to fight this world to survive"; and other-worldly behaviour: "I have to create another world to survive".'

As adults, says Yapp, we tend to judge children only by what we see, rather than by trying to understand what underlies their behaviour. We will forgive ourselves for behaving badly when we are under stress, but judge children much more severely. *We* are basically good people having a lapse; *they* are basically bad children, who occasionally fail to annoy. Children may put up façades of being clever and strong – taking risks, running across motorways, getting what they want by stealing or fighting, acting as if they need nobody, are invulnerable. This behaviour has to be tackled, but there is also the need to get at the root cause of the feelings which lead to it.[30] The essence of such work, says Yapp, is to realize that the children are themselves unhappy with the difficult situation they have got into, and can respond to someone who is trying to look for a way out with them. Faith and trust that even the most unlovely are made in God's image and have the capacity to love are fundamental family values. For it is an act of faith to believe in any core of humanity in the most destructive and disruptive children, and it may in the end not be possible to get through. But those who work with these children and young people have many stories to tell of what can begin to happen when their trust is won.

It also makes a difference in ordinary parenting to believe that children have a core of goodness and a desire to please. It is very easy to jump from a specific behaviour in a child, say hitting out, to thinking of the child as violent. Yet children absorb their parents' fears that they are full of evil and need strict control, and parental beliefs about this have a profound effect on children: 'our unconscious, on the basis of how we interpreted to ourselves our early experiences with our parents, causes us to believe either that the world is basically accepting and approving of us, or rejecting and disapproving'. It determines whether or not we feel lovable.[31]This should warn us against allowing the notion of original sin too great a part in our dealings with children, for it is likely to instil in them a sense of worthlessness and lack of confidence. This may make them quicker to rely on God for salvation, but tends to produce conformity, and often leaves Christians stuck in the early stages of faith, unwilling to take responsibility for moral living and spiritual growth.

A baby, then, is born with the capacity for both good and evil, and with the right kind of parenting and education, the good capacities can predominate, and the destructiveness can be manageable. The idea of 'original sin' makes most sense when it is related to the way we learn about, and choose between, right and wrong. It is fascinating to watch the emergence of sin in children. Each child seems to have their own fall, a point at which they understand something is wrong, know they shouldn't do it, but go ahead anyway. As babies and toddlers, they do things they shouldn't, but they are not deliberately weighing up right and wrong. The fourteen-month old keeps reaching out for the electric socket to see what happens, not to be defiant. But at the age of two or three, you can see them thinking: 'I know I'm wrong, but I just don't care.' It's also arguable (with Piaget and others) that this is an essential stage for everyone if they are to go on to develop moral maturity. If that is the case, should we be following those theologians who through Christian history have spoken of the Fall as told in Genesis as a Fall upwards – not the coming of evil into the world, but the coming of the choice that enables us to be truly good?

In order to grow up, we have to discover for ourselves what life means: 'The moral option we face is not a choice between obedience and disobedience. There is only one moral choice: to disobey, to eat of the tree of knowledge, and thereafter to live through the hardships of life.' The Bible, says Soelle, calls us to choose freedom over against childlike obedience: 'to journey out into the world despite our intense longing to remain home and to forfeit our adulthood'. Christianity traditionally supports this longing to escape and 'go home' to the garden.[32] This call to grow up and leave behind dependency on a paternalistic father or God is a common one among recent writers, and it is important in a Church which has not fully grasped the meaning of being adult disciples. The danger is that people's dependency needs are written off as entirely inappropriate, whereas they too are important. We need other people, to be intimate with them and bound to them. We are not to depend on them for the whole of our identity, and yet if our bonds with them are real, we will be diminished by their death or going away.

Carol Harrison offers some interesting insights into this in her study of early Christian writers. She refers to the minority view that Adam and Eve were created as immature children, innocent and naïve. God would have let them eat of the tree of knowledge in due course, when they were mature enough to do so. It is their immaturity and naïvety which allows them to fall into temptation. They become suddenly adult before their time, and aware of their nakedness. Harrison suggests that 'Adam and Eve are archetypes for humanity because what happened in paradise is what is going on all the time. All . . . when born or baptized, have the potential for perfection but their human life is so hedged about with limitations and overshadowed by the unavoidable presence of evil that it is almost impossible . . . not to sin.'[33] Though there are problems with this view, as Harrison notes, it does have echoes in a world where we speak of children growing old too quickly, faced with experiences that they are not mature enough to understand or handle. The difficulty lies in the implicit assumption that childhood is about innocence, and represents an ideal state to be returned to. This might suggest that children should be protected for as long as possible. An alternative is that children should be helped earlier rather than later to make moral choices, to understand the world around them, as appropriate to their age. Protection of the young has its place, but this must not be overdone, lest it leaves children too vulnerable in their innocence.

Notes

1. Quoted in L. De Mause, ed., *The History of Childhood* (New York, Harper & Row, 1975), pp. 137-8.

2. Quoted in M. Phillips, ed., *The Parent Trap* (Guardian Studies, Vol. 4, 1991), p. 19.

3. With apologies to Stevie Smith, who originally spoke of 'Not waving, but drowning!'

4. See, for example, P. Aries, *Centuries of Childhood* (London, Jonathan Cape, 1962); De Mause, ed., *The History of Childhood*; and the critique offered of them by Lawrence Stone, in P. Barnes et al., eds, *Personality, Development and Learning* (London, Hodder & Stoughton/Open University Press, 1984). Also, see the more accessible C. Hardyment, *Dream Babies* (London, Jonathan Cape, 1983), and B. Ehrenreich and D. English, *For Her Own Good* (London, Pluto Press, 1979).

5. See, for example, D. Archard, *Children: Rights and Childhood* (London, Routledge, 1993).

6. Hardyment, *Dream Babies*, p. 174. Hardyment reveals that Watson's own children turned out perfectly healthy and happy despite this. However, Watson's wife seems to have been a sensible woman who didn't follow his instructions to the letter, and kissed the children when he wasn't looking!

7. Hardyment, *Dream Babies*, p. 226.

8. Ehrenreich and English see some significance in the films of the period that allied children with the devil – like *Rosemary's Baby* (1968) and *The Exorcist* (1973). I'm not sure that very much can be made of this, though it is interesting to note the way that films of the late 1980s and 1990s have developed a theme of parental

or adult inadequacy in coping with babies or children who are strong enough to cope alone – e.g. *Three Men and a Baby*, or *Home Alone*.

9. J. Dobson, *Dare to Discipline* (Wheaton: Illinois, Tyndale House Publishers, 1970 [first British edition 1972]); *The New Dare to Discipline* (Eastbourne, Kingsway, 1993). See also Andrew Graystone's useful critique of Dobson, 'Dare to Disagree', *Third Way*, April 1991.

10. B. Friedan, *The Feminine Mystique* (Harmondsworth, Penguin Books, 1963), p. 167.

11. I refer to the literature, which includes both specialist childrearing books and magazines. Though not all parents will read this for themselves, they are likely to be influenced by it through what they hear from doctors, health visitors, social workers or other parents.

12. C. Steiner, *Scripts People Live* (London, Grove Press, 1974), p. 367.

13. Quoted in Phillips, ed., *The Parent Trap*, p. 8.

14. B. Bettelheim, *A Good Enough Parent* (London, Thames & Hudson, 1987), pp. 105, and 114. Bettelheim says he uses 'parent/ he' to mean mother as well as father, but I don't find that usage terribly helpful given that there's an issue concerning the role of the father and respect for the father which is lost when the male referent is taken as generic.

15. M. Herbert, *Discipline* (Oxford, Basil Blackwell, 1989), pp. 28-9.

16. Ortlund, *Disciplines of the Home* (Milton Keynes, Word UK, 1990), pp. 93ff. She gives the biblical reference of Titus 3.2 – a slightly dubious interpretation of it, I have to say, though it could be a popular one among members of a government!

17. Ortlund, *Disciplines of the Home*, p. 55.

18. M. Kennedy, 'Christianity – Help or Hindrance for the Abused Child or Adult?', *Child Abuse Review*, Vol. 5, No. 3, 1991/2. See also H. Cashman, *Christianity and Child Sexual Abuse* (London, SPCK, 1993).

19. K. and J. McGinnis, *Parenting for Peace and Justice – Ten Years Later* (Maryknoll, New York, Orbis Books, 1990), p. 25.

20. B. Spock, *Parenting* (London, Michael Joseph, 1989), pp. 135ff. I do not know if a group of girls or a mixed group would behave very differently, but I suspect not.

21. V. Satir, *Peoplemaking* (California, Science and Behaviour Books, 1972), p. 210.

22. Ortlund, *Disciplines of the Home*, p. 131. She does not say whether other people's children matter.

23. 'Would God Use the Rod?' *Guardian*, 11 May 1993.

24. *Horizon*, BBC Television, 23 May 1993.

25. *Observer*, 25 April 1993.

26. M. Frampton, in an MTh. dissertation submitted to King's College London in 1980, p. 47.

27. Frampton, MTh. dissertation, p. 56.

28. Spock, *Parenting*, p. 265.

29. *Observer* 28 March 1993. Coward draws heavily on a conversation with Margaret Rustin, and the idea that constructive and destructive elements are side by side in the personality is a common one for psychoanalysts. For example, Melanie Klein's work is relevant here.

30. N. Yapp, *My Problem Child* (Harmondsworth, Penguin Books, 1991), pp. 52 and 126-7. There remains the problem of how to deal with children like this in casual encounters, or if you are a victim of them.

31. Bettelheim, *A Good Enough Parent*, p. 12.

32. D. Soelle with S. Cloyes, *To Work and to Love* (Philadelphia, Fortress Press, 1984), p. 75.

33. C. Harrison, 'The Childhood of Man in Early Christian Writers', *Augustinianum*, June 1992, p. 75.

chapter eight

Reconstructing
Family Values

*In parenthood, as in business, politics and war, the corr-
elation between the efforts of the people in charge and the
results, whether dazzling or disastrous, is negligible.*

Katherine Whitehorn[1]

*Our delegated power over our children is the power to
free them, the power to serve them, the power to teach
them the truth. This is the power of love which can flow
through us from God.*

Two parents[2]

*You are the people of God; he loved you and chose you
for his own. So then, you must clothe yourselves with
compassion, kindness, humility, gentleness, and patience.
Be tolerant with one another and forgive one another
whenever any of you has a complaint against someone
else. You must forgive one another just as the Lord has
forgiven you. And to all these qualities add love, which
binds all things together in perfect unity.*

Col. 3.12 -14

Gospel values

One of the central themes of this book is the need to affirm the
values which support family life and relationships. Christian
writing about parenting has often looked for proof texts which can
be applied - particularly popular are references to the necessity for

children to honour, respect, and obey their parents. There are a number of other texts which make a different point, however, and it is interesting that even those who quote the Bible on family life most often do not take much account of these other passages. Jesus' attitude to children included his saying, 'Let the children come to me and do not stop them, because the Kingdom of heaven belongs to such as these' (Matt.19.14). And, 'if anyone should cause one of these little ones to lose his faith in me, it would be better for that person to have a large millstone tied round his neck and be drowned in the deep sea' (Matt. 18.6). Paul balances his instructions to children to obey their parents by adding: 'Parents do not irritate your children, or they will become discouraged' (Col. 3.21) and 'Parents, do not treat your children in such a way as to make them angry' (Eph. 6.4). Dobson uses the J. B. Phillips version, 'Fathers, do not over-correct your children', which gives this verse a different slant. The parental task for writers such as Dobson includes instructing and judging, yet one of the things which most often irritates, discourages, and provokes children to anger is the feeling that they are constantly being watched and judged. As adults, we have the same reaction, of course, when faced with a superior (or even a spouse) who thinks we can never do anything right.

In any case, biblical teaching on childrearing is not to be found simply in the texts which mention parents or children, but in the core of the gospel message. Children are to be treated with at least the same care which we owe to our neighbours in general, loved as we love ourselves. The command to 'be tender, compassionate, forgiving one another as God in Christ forgave you' must apply to the relations between parents and children if families are to reflect the values of the gospel. The fruits of the Spirit are to be sought in family interactions: love, joy, peace, patience, kindness, goodness, gentleness, faithfulness, self-control. It is striking that we so seldom apply texts like these to children or family life, for they challenge many of our perceptions of the parental role. And yet, there are problems in saying this, for it so easily becomes either a pious cliché or an extra burden to make people (and especially mothers) feel guilty about their lack of patience under difficult circumstances. However, it is worth persevering with the attempt to outline a different set of 'family values', if only because they contrast noticeably with traditional family values, which stress such things as control, punishment, obedience, and respect for authority.

Empathy

One of the mainstays of good parenting is the ability to empathize with children. Without it, neither kindness nor discipline (in the sense of limit-setting) is possible. This entails remembering what it felt like to be a child: to go to a new school, to fall in love, to be afraid of the dark. Empathy, says Bettelheim, requires 'that one consider the other person an equal – not in regard to knowledge, intelligence, or experience, and certainly not in maturity, but in respect to thé feelings which motivate us all'.[3] It is acknowledging the strength of a child's feelings, and the fact that they *matter* which is important here. It is very easy to dismiss a child's fears because we know they are groundless, forgetting how overwhelming those fears are to them. Children may not have exactly the same reactions that their parents had as children, but if parents are in touch with their own experience, they will be in a better position to take their children's anxieties seriously. Empathy should not lead to a takeover bid for the child's experience, but to attentive listening to what they really feel – and a willingness not to intrude where the child wishes to be private.

The importance of listening to children is stressed in nearly all books about childrearing. In some respects, this is a contradictory value to assertiveness, which involves repeatedly stating one's own needs over against someone who is arguing, rather than trying to hear what they are actually saying. Yet these are both skills which have a place in particular circumstances, for attentive listening should not be seen as something which requires the denial of all self-interest. Full attention is not always possible, but relationships can only thrive if there are some moments when real communication can happen. The fact that parents have a disciplinary role in relation to children means that it is all too easy to criticize and express blame when things go wrong in the child's life, in a way they would never do with their friends. Bettelheim quotes the biblical injunction to lift the downtrodden, and points out how often we fail to lift our children's spirits, but instead aggravate them by criticism, or by minimizing their griefs and sorrows in order to spare ourselves. One response to all this is to say that listening and verbal articulation of feelings are middle-class values, and have no relevance to working-class family life. It may be true that the way these things happen varies according to social class and the particular culture a family belongs to, but empathy and communication are values which cross all boundaries. Such values have always been the marks of good family life, and there is plenty of evidence that families from all social groups find them important.

However, being able to empathize and communicate are skills that do not come naturally to everyone – and often men seem to find it harder than women. The way women generally talk and listen fits more easily into relationships with children, although those who have had difficult upbringings themselves can experience problems in relating empathetically to their children. This is illustrated in the study by Belenky et al. of women of various classes and ethnic origins. They observe that mothers who have been beaten as children cannot imagine ways of teaching and influencing their children other than by violence; and mothers who have little sense of their own identity and voices find it hard to draw out their children's voices. Indeed, such mothers were likely to regard their children's curious questioning as disrespect, talking back. But as these women began to find themselves, so they discovered that they were able to respond differently to their children. It is, then, not always simple for parents to be empathetic – it may take time and help. The emphasis on talking to children as people in their own right makes the relationships of some parents and children much easier, but may create new stresses for others. However, as Belenky et al. conclude: 'Ultimately, it is the receiving of the child and hearing what he or she has to say that develops the child's mind and personhood. . . . Parents who enter into a dialogue with their children, who draw out and respect their opinions, are more likely to have children whose intellectual and ethical development proceeds rapidly and surely.'[4]

Empathy and understanding are granted more readily to babies and small children than to older ones. Studies of parents of young children show them searching for explanations of difficult behaviour – is it tiredness, teething, jealousy of a new baby?

Older children are less often excused. Their irritability or whining or disruptive behaviour is often attributed to their being awkward by nature, rather than reactions to what is going on in their lives. Though as adults we know that worry makes us snap at people, or prone to accidents, we less often stop to think that children's difficult behaviour has an explanation, because, after all, that is what children are like. One reason why children can continue to be bullied at school or abused by a neighbour is because parents interpret poor work at school or reluctance to visit as typical childish or teenage behaviour. And indeed, it is hard to read such subtle signs accurately – it is often only in hindsight that the symptoms can be recognized for what they are. However, it is important to be alert to what these signs might mean, especially if children might be harming themselves – for example, with drugs or an eating disorder, or getting into trouble with the police.

If a child is unconsciously acting out unacknowledged conflict within a family system, early understanding of why this is happening may enable problems to be resolved before they get out of hand. This was graphically illustrated in a television programme about a five-year-old boy who was destructive and out of control. Work with the family showed how his behaviour had deteriorated after the death of his much-loved grandfather, and reflected his mother's repressed grief. Other steps were needed to help the family too, but understanding how the behaviour had originated was an important step in dealing with it. This is where a 'systems' approach to families comes into its own. It challenges the tendency to look for simple ideas about who is to blame, concentrating instead on the interaction within a family system.[5] As I showed in the last chapter, this has implications for dealing with disruptive children, whose behaviour often has its own strange internal logic.

Compassion belongs alongside empathy and understanding, as another 'gospel value'. It is a characteristic ascribed to God and to Christ, a pity which yearns to reach out to those in distress, to embrace the prodigal son. Practising compassion in ordinary family life may mean taking a gentler approach, recognizing how inexperienced children are in dealing with the world and their feelings. It may mean being less judgemental about, say, the father who walks out on his family, recognizing the strains which were tearing him apart. Yet compassion may also be allied to firm action – compassion for the jealous child who harms a baby, or the alcoholic uncle who becomes violent, does not stand in the way of acting to limit the damage, or of invoking consequences which may include punishment. I shall look in more detail at issues to do with punishment and control in the next chapter.

The critical eye

Although children may be perceived, and some may actually be, out of control in public, many of them are subject to a lot of critical attention in their homes. Many parents regard it as their duty to socialize children, teach them how to behave, and this clearly is part of the role. However, this can result in constant criticism, which actually has little effect on negative behaviour, and can prevent children from learning positive skills. We have probably all had the experience of messing up something we are perfectly capable of doing, because someone happens to be watching. Yet parents frequently subject their children to that critical attention: 'Don't drop it, be careful, oh look what you've done, you stupid child, you're so careless.' Why is it that children rarely seem to have the genuine accidents we adults have? Mistakes are part of the learning process, and we all need freedom to make them.

Despite the fears that permissiveness has taken over, the message many parents still need to hear is 'lighten up'. Stanway suggests that families which make demands on children to be 'perfect' 'leave children so prone to failure they can be made to feel guilty about almost anything', through into their adult lives.[6] The Church's teaching can reinforce this, and Christian parents trying to impose godly standards may be particularly prone to producing guilt – one parent suggested to me that what set a Christian parent aside was that they regarded children's wrong-doing as sins against God. But this is a very heavy burden to lay on a child. Instead, concentrating on looking for good things to affirm in children's behaviour not only reinforces good behaviour, but is theologically appropriate. If the people of God are to be joyful, and take pleasure in God's creation, so too should children know that they are a genuine delight to their parents. Perhaps joy is another family value to be encouraged, even though where life is harsh, it may only be possible to glimpse it for short moments.

In the wider world, attitudes to young offenders also show severity and a quickness to judge. There is public outcry that so many of them only get cautioned – and yet over 80 per cent of those who are cautioned for a first offence do not reoffend. The minority who repeatedly offend need a different treatment, but being heavy-handed about first offences makes criminality out of youthful error. Clearly, parents will have their own definitions of what actually matters and what doesn't, but it is important to be selective about what battles are joined. Many of the irritating behaviours of young children, and the antisocial conduct of teenagers, are phases that will pass. Like office filing which can be discarded as out of date if it is left long enough, many of the irritating behaviours children have will pass with time, and do not really merit constant nagging. One day they will want to wash their hair; in a few years' time, the house will seem empty without their music. The trouble is that some of the behaviours that teenagers today try out are either addictive (like smoking or hard drugs), or lethal (like 'joyriding'), or both, and such teenagers may not survive to pass through the phase as their parents passed through being football hooligans or stealing sweets from Woolworth's. The further problem for society is that it makes no difference to the victim whether they are hurt by someone's first offence or their twentieth, especially if there is a constant supply of first offenders.

Children are often labelled stupid, lazy, or naughty, and it can become a self-fulfilling prophecy. When they make errors, they may be subject to sarcasm, ridicule, or severe punishment. Such attitudes are not confined to family life – superiors can be found treating their subordinates in this way in all sorts of settings. The bullying boss and the sarcastic teacher, are well-known figures. But Christians should be seeking to treat others with the same mercy God shows us. In this context, it is worth considering the parable of the Unforgiving Servant in Matthew 18 – perhaps changing the wording to, 'If my child keeps on sinning against me, how many times do I have to forgive them?' We may want to argue that the situations are quite different, and that the parable does not apply to parents, who have to be stern to teach children a lesson. But why do we think that is different from God's treatment of us? If we can be forgiven for negligence, weakness, and our own deliberate fault, can we not then show mercy to others, including children?

Accepting individuality

Parental attitudes to this are influenced by whether they see themselves as moulding the child into the correct form, or providing an appropriate atmosphere in which a child may flourish and develop their own unique identity. Accepting a child's uniqueness is not always as easy as it ought to be. Parents have their own dreams of what they want for, and from, their children. A child with a disability may throw parental expectations into confusion in a very stark way – and yet once the child can be seen as a unique individual with their own contribution to the family's life, many parents will say: 'we could not imagine life without them'.[7] Every child brings its own personalities and gifts to a family. There may be a clash between parent and child which disrupts the family, but, equally, an easy-going or humorous child can make life easier for everyone. That children have different personalities can be evident from the moment of birth, and the way a child develops is a product of the interaction with their parents as well as with their life circumstances.

It is a failing of much childcare literature that not enough account is taken of such differences in the temperament of parents and children, or the differing home circumstances in which they live. Yet not only do social considerations, like housing, make a difference to how a child develops, but so too do gender, birth order, social class, ethnicity, and colour. There can be no one right way for parents to proceed given these variables. Even 'do as you would be done by' is not necessarily good advice, given that different personality types relate to the world outside them in very different ways, as the Myers-Briggs and other 'temperament sorters' show.[8] As Anne Bradstreet, a seventeenth-century writer, put it: 'Diverse children have their different natures . . . those parents are wise that can fit their nurture according to their Nature.'[9]

139

A parent's acceptance of their child's uniqueness and eccentricities may make it more likely that the child will accept the parent's uniqueness and eccentricity. After all, we generally do not choose our parents, and we are bound to end up with ones who are a little bit odd. Kelly asserts hopefully in *The Mother's Almanac* that 'Fortunately most children accept our fallibility as well as our love.'[10] An emphasis on children's rights to good parenting can become dangerous if it does not recognize that no parenting is perfect. Parents are not gods, whose love, gratefully received, will protect children from harm and bring only blessing. Even God does not promise a pain-free existence. The good-enough parent will influence for some harm as well as good – that is inevitable; but they will also be on the child's side whatever happens.

For one of children's needs is to have parents who will not give them up, who are faithful to them, dependable in the sense that children know that their needs will be met. This is not the same thing as having parents who are organized and who always do exactly as they say they will. Households manage things in different ways, and some people set little store by keeping to plans. Children can learn to live with parental idiosyncrasies – although being let down by a parent on something highly important to a child can hurt very deeply. It is particularly difficult, however, for children who never know how parents will behave – if a parent is alcoholic or erratically violent, for example. Chronic illness, depression, conflict between parents, worries at work, racism, can all make parents less capable of being supportive. When such situations are prolonged, and children feel they have no one they can depend on, it can cause long-term damage. It is the fact that parents can no longer be relied on to provide a secure world which contributes to the hurt that children suffer when their parents are in conflict or get divorced.

It should also be said that where parents themselves feel insecure and lacking in confidence, it is harder for them to provide the dependability children need. In a rapidly changing world, with all the pressures faced by adults and children alike, and a climate in which parents are blamed for the ills of society, it is not surprising if many parents feel they have lost their way. The things which worked for previous generations are not always appropriate now – for example, because of traffic and the (rare) risk of abduction, children cannot be left as free to explore the world on their own. As more is uncovered about children's developmental needs, the expectations on parents are higher, and there are increasing numbers of people telling them what to do or not to do. We are not certain as adults that we can create and sustain a decent society, and we are conscious that we cannot offer our children much hope for the future.

Children who go irretrievably wrong pose their own set of questions for their families. Should parents (or indeed other family members) cut themselves off from a child who commits murder? To what extent are they to blame? What can they ever say to that other family torn apart by their offspring's action? The limits of parental acceptance are tested here. Yet where parenting is modelled on God's relation to humankind, maintaining a bond in spite of everything is what counts. As Jürgen Moltmann explains:

> God is for me; I am his child. Christ is beside me; I am his brother. Whether this makes me believe more strongly or whether I doubt all the more, whether I am swallowed up in the darkness of night or find myself at the dawn of a new day – I know: there is someone waiting for me, who will not give me up, who goes ahead of me, who lifts me up, someone to whom I am important.[11]

Most parents will not experience the trauma of having a child go publicly, disastrously wrong. A great many, however, will attach a lot of importance to the way their children behave in public. If we were asked what our parents most wanted of us as a child, or if parents are asked what they want of their children, the immediate answers might well be in terms of being happy, having faith, finding a good job and marriage partner. The most honest answer, however, boils down to this: that children should not embarrass their parents in public. (Actually, the most desperate desire of children is that their parents should not embarrass *them* in public!) In the home, parents will tolerate a certain amount of difficult behaviour, but in school, church, and the street, most parents still want their children to reflect well on them, to feel in control of their behaviour. The present government's emphasis on parental responsibilities and choice keys into our gut feelings about this: the good parent has children who are well behaved, parents should be able to control their children. This seems to be true across different social groups – pride in how children turn out, and pressure not to give the family a bad name in the neighbourhood, are strong values in working-class communities, for example. The activities of antisocial young men, for which parents are blamed, may well cause acute distress. However, in some instances, where a community feels itself to be in conflict with the authorities, or families have a long association with crime, such behaviour may be a source of pride.

An emphasis on conformity and obedience may be particularly characteristic of Christian parenting, for good children show their parents to be good Christians. As I pointed out in *A Woman's Work*, this is especially true for mothers, when their main role in life is seen as raising godly children. In many churches, despite all the emphasis on all-age worship and family services, the onus is on parents to keep younger children quiet and well behaved for at least some parts of the service. The effectiveness of Christian parents may be judged by how long their teenage children keep coming to church – those who play a full part in church life or, even better, go into full-time Christian ministry, allow their parents to feel secretly superior to parents whose children rebel.

Yet as children grow older, there is a need to define themselves over against their parents, and not fitting in with parental expectations may be part of this. As I shall point out in Chapter 10, this poses acute difficulties for devout children of Christian parents, who must somehow separate themselves in order to know their faith as their own. Stanway comments that adolescents who are working out self-determination may throw values around rather as a toddler does food or toys, hoping unknowingly that parents will pick up the pieces. Adolescents 'need their parents to maintain their values, but not to take too active a role in asserting them'. They need, he says, to define their selves against parental approval, for fear parents will dictate their personality. In such situations, parents need to hold on to their own values, accept adolescent behaviour without approving of it, but not disapproving so strongly that their teenagers cannot give it up. In the meantime, they must offer unrestricted love and welcome.[12] Conflict of this sort is not inevitable, but when it happens, it does not represent failure. The transition to adulthood, like birth, may be a painful process, but it is usually productive pain.

Living with conflict

Children of any age may behave badly not because of underlying problems, but simply in order to test out boundaries. This kind of behaviour seems to be more readily recognized by writers such as Dobson who take seriously the idea of children's wilful defiance. I am not sure I would use this language (or Dobson's solutions), but it is important to recognize that it is natural for human beings to want at times to know what they can get away with. The idea implicit in many childrearing books that parents can avoid getting into conflict if they are sufficiently understanding, misses out this dimension.

It has not always been easy for Christians to come to terms with this, for our ideal of family life is one of harmony and co-operation. The 1988 Lambeth Conference statement saw the family as the place

> where one can begin to experience and understand love, compassion, and deep personal relationship with God. It is where individuals – brothers, sisters, parents and other members – learn to grow and work together. Here one can gain a foretaste of all the peoples of God's creation coming together to achieve a unity of mutual purpose and service. . . . The family is . . . the place where roles are defined, where the lines of responsibility and freedom are drawn, where sexual relationships are modelled, where mutual respect, order and discipline are taught. . . . In healthy families, children and adults are nourished and cherished; dependent members, whether disabled children or adults, are protected and valued; the wisdom and experience of the elderly is cherished and utilised; and individuals experience in family life nothing less than the love of the Father, 'from whom every family in heaven and earth is named' (Eph. 3.15).[13]

This may be a description of much that is good in family life, but it has no place for conflict and passion. It is not simply that real family life is not like that, cannot live up to the ideal, but that this is inadequate as an ideal.

I noted in *Distorted Images* that one problem with Christian descriptions of sexual relationships is that they lack passion and earthiness, and descriptions of family life have a similar failing. The slamming doors are not sinful interruptions to our attempts at godly family living, but part and parcel of what it means to live together as family. It is interesting that the McGinnises, reviewing their thoughts about family life ten years on, suggest that they now see that conflict is a norm in family life, not an exception to what should be a hassle-free existence. This came home to me during an altercation with one of my children, when I was trying to be fair-minded and to discover what lay behind the problem. Yet clearly this approach was not what was required; it was too detached. What was needed was for me to be angry and passionate: 'Don't you *dare* do that again, I couldn't bear it if anything happened to you.' The fact that we can make people angry is a sign that we matter to them, and allowing it to show does not have to be sinful. The great danger in saying that is that anger misused can be abusive and can lead to violence. Like sexual desire, it is a passion which can go astray – but it can also be an important part of the bonds between people. This is clearly illustrated in Terri Apter's work on the relationships between mothers and daughters. Apter shows teenage girls in a constant battle to define their own identity over against their mothers' views of who they are. Yet this is not a struggle to separate from their mothers, but to renegotiate a valued bond with them.[14]

Conflict, passion, anger, and difference, rightly acknowledged, can be part of a healthy family system in which individual family members develop. The same is true in the wider world. The attempt to bring all together in peace and harmony stops us seeing the reality of the differences which divide us. Toleration and acceptance of difference do need to be pursued, but we have to recognize that some divisions cannot be bridged. We have to find ways forward which allow us to live with those tensions, rather than denying them for the sake of Christian unity.

Perhaps the fact that these values are part of family living, alongside those of compassion and empathy, is what saves 'gospel values' from being oppressive. There are a range of values which will need stressing at different times according to our different circumstances. But starting with the need to see children as unique beings, deserving of respect and understanding, leads us in a different direction from beginning with obedience, control, and punishment. As Christ himself showed in his teaching, rules about conduct and punishment do not come first – rather, the first commandment is to love God and others as we are loved. It is in that context that issues of control and limit setting must be looked at, and this is the theme of the next chapter.

Notes

1. *Observer*, 3 August 1986.

2. Two parents, quoted in K. and J. McGinnis, *Parenting for Peace and Justice - Ten Years Later* (Maryknoll, New York, Orbis Books, 1990).

3. B. Bettelheim, *A Good Enough Parent* (London, Thames & Hudson, 1987), p. 88.

4. M. Belenky et al., *Women's Ways of Knowing* (New York, Basic Books, 1986), p. 189.

5. For a helpful discussion of this, see S. Walrond-Skinner, *The Fulcrum and the Fire* (London, Darton, Longman & Todd, 1993). She also looks at the question of ensuring that people like abusers take responsibility for their actions, so that understanding does not become excuse.

6. A. Stanway, *Preparing for Life* (London, Viking, 1988), p. 228.

7. See Chapter 7 of A. Phoenix, A. Woollett, and E. Lloyd, eds, *Motherhood* (London, Sage, 1991) for a discussion of disability in family life.

8. I am indebted to Hilary Thompson for this point. See D. Keirsey and M. Bates, *Please Understand Me* (Del Mar, California, Prometheus Nemesis Book Company, 1984) for an introduction to Myers-Briggs, including discussion of temperament in children.

9. Quoted in L. De Mause, *The History of Childhood* (New York, Harper & Row, 1975), p. 349.

10. M. Kelly, *The Mother's Almanac* (New York, Doubleday, 1989), p. 280.

11. J. Moltmann, *Experiences of God* (Philadelphia, Fortress Press, 1980), p. 5.

12. Stanway, *Preparing for Life*, pp. 156ff.

13. *The Truth Shall Make you Free*, pp. 185-6.

14. T. Apter, *Altered Loves* (London, Harvester Wheatsheaf, 1990).

chapter nine

The Ethics of Parental
Intervention, or the
'Just Smack'Theory

*We are born into other people's intentions. We learn our
names and our natures at their hands, and they cannot
teach us more truth than they know or will freely tell.*

<u>Theodore Roszak</u>[1]

*Discipline without forgiveness is brutal; forgiveness with-
out discipline is cheap.*

<u>Calvin</u>[2]

*Frequent yet not severe whippings do them good . . . And
this should continue not only while they are three, four,
or five years old but as long as they have need of it up to
the age of twenty-five.*

<u>A fifteenth-century Dominican friar</u> [3]

The question of control and punishment is one which has emerged
at many different points in this book. It concerns the way in which
parents discipline their children, the treatment of offenders in
society, and the discipline imposed by the Church on those who
are sinners. I am using a slightly different perspective in my
examination of these issues in this chapter, which looks at the
ethics of parental intervention – in other words, when parents
ought to intervene in the lives of their children, and whether
physical punishment or coercion is appropriate. The first part of
this chapter began life as a lecture to the Oxford Ministry Course

on the 'just smack' Theory – a term I coined to parallel the idea of the 'just war' which we had previously been examining.

The rights of parents

Underlying this theme is the question of parental and children's rights, something which has been a key issue in public debate in Britain, especially following the implementation of the Children Act. Headlines about children divorcing parents, and whether parents or childminders can smack, reflect this debate. It should be said that the idea that children have individual rights within the family is a new and Western one, made possible both by affluence and by a philosophy of individualism. The context of this chapter is therefore even more firmly rooted in British (or Western) culture, in an attempt to respond to these issues – though there may be some points which can have a wider application.

In the past, parents were assumed to have certain rights in relation to their children, but the key concept in the 1989 Children Act is parental responsibility. One commentator writes that the Act assumes that 'bringing up children is the responsibility of their parents and that the State's principal role is to help rather than to interfere. . . . "parental responsibility" . . . covers the whole bundle of duties towards the child, with their concomitant powers and authority over him [sic], together with some procedural rights to protection against interference'.[4] The child's welfare is 'paramount', though this can cause conflict with the principles of non-interference. If no one is going to intervene, the parent can get away with behaviour which may damage the child.

A child can only be taken away from its parents if it is suffering, or is likely to suffer, significant harm. It is obvious in some cases that harm is being done – for example, where sexual or physical abuse is occurring. In other cases, it is a delicate matter of judgement. A child's home life may be damaging, but is it more so than the damage that would result from going into care? The first year of the operation of the Children Act saw a dramatic fall in the number of children taken into care and put on the At Risk register. It is difficult to know whether this is a matter for celebration, because much less abuse is going on, or because

149

over-officious social workers have had their power curbed; or whether more cases of abuse are slipping through the net.

There are also questions here about the other factors which come into play when social workers or others assess a child's home life. Families may be judged inadequate when their child-rearing patterns differ from white middle-class ideals. Thus New and David believe that the reluctance to take children into care 'is far more readily overcome when the "inadequate" families are poor or black or are headed by a lone mother'. In other words, some mothers are more liable to state intervention based on their structural position rather than because they are inadequate.[5] The Child Support Act is a massive piece of intervention by the state into domestic life, applying particularly to single mothers on low incomes. If they wish to draw benefits, they are required (with a few exceptions) to name the father of their child, and the Child Support Agency has powers to track down errant fathers. The principle of holding absent fathers responsible for their children is a good one, but unfortunately the process does nothing to relieve these mothers' poverty or to help them to become independent. In practice, it seems that the truly irresponsible fathers are not the ones who are tracked down, but those who are already paying some maintenance, or who acknowledge their children. Some orders for maintenance previously agreed by parents are being set aside, and towards the end of 1993, the government was recognizing the need for a review of how the system had been operating.

There are some tensions in recent legislation between the understandings of parental responsibility and children's needs. It is almost as if 'parental responsibility' is a stick with which to beat parents, whilst 'parental choice' is given to good parents. Parental choice is central to the government's education policy, but there is nothing about the interests of the child being important. Children are the actual consumers of education, yet have no formal say in what is provided. The point is not that 'children's choice' is necessarily desirable, but that children and parents are treated rather differently in the two areas of legislation. Similarly, if a child commits a criminal offence, their treatment will be dictated by the 1991 Criminal Justice Act, which has a punishment ethos, rather than making the child's welfare paramount. Parents can be held to account for offences committed by children under the age of sixteen, which is a positive step in the case of parents who make no attempt to deter their children's criminal activity. But it provides no help where children are out of control and their parents at their wits' end *because* they feel their responsibility.

Many religious people, as well as those on the political Right, place a lot of emphasis on parental choice in the area of sex education. There is marked disagreement between those who argue that sex education has led to increases in promiscuity and teenage pregnancy, and those who argue that these problems have arisen because there is too little of it. Organizations such as Family and Youth Concern are particularly emphatic about their opposition to current sex education in schools, and pressure from such quarters influenced new legislation in 1993 to allow parents to withdraw their children from sex education classes. There has been concern expressed about this – for example, by the Sex Education Forum (an umbrella body for a broad range of groups with an interest in children, health, and sex education), which believes that children have a right to information about sex. They point out that a majority of parents and teenagers are in favour of sex education in schools. Carol Lee, who works in sex education herself, objects to the idea that parents have the right to instruct their child about sex according to their own values, for this can be in tension with the child's own interests. It is also partly a question of individual rights versus the interests of society – parents cannot have an entirely free choice about their children's schooling, for example, where long-term plans have to be made about schools, class sizes, and so on. It may be in a teenager's interest to have access to contraception, even if parents do not agree.

Victoria Gillick, who took a high profile stand on this issue in the 1980s, tried to establish parents' rights to supervise the physical and moral welfare of their children, though she was eventually defeated. But parents' rights lessen with the maturity of their children. Those under eighteen are regarded as having some autonomy, and the (somewhat arbitrary) sequence of age-related legislation indicates this. They can consent to their own medical treatment if they are mature, and children over the age of ten can be held responsible for criminal acts. Churches regard children as mature enough to make faith commitments through confirmation or baptism from as early as seven, though more usually this happens in the early teens. In this context, Lee has a point when she notes that 'religious feeling is based on the notion that there is an individual soul and that each individual is capable not only of working out what is right and wrong, but of acting on this. There is no point in saving an individual soul if the soul is not individual, and learning to be a moral, discerning person does not begin at 16.'[6] This is an area which needs more debate, since the emphasis for Christians has generally been on how we can instil our values in children, rather than on how we might encourage moral development in them.

Ethics in childrearing – the example of force-feeding

If children in the past were regarded as the property of their parents, things today are different. One parent summed it up by saying: 'I do not own my children. I own the responsibility for them, and this is given back when they get older.'[7] Legally, parents are responsible for making sure their children are adequately clothed, fed, educated, and protected; but there is a huge range of behaviour within that area by which parents can exercise power over their children's lives. Clearly, parents need to guide and care for their children, set reasonable limits, and be responsible. There are questions, though, about the way in which this is done, and the way children are treated. For example, does a responsibility to ensure a child is adequately fed mean it is permissible to force-feed it? There is very little attention given to such ethical issues in childrearing. Though the *New Dictionary of Christian Ethics* states that 'Child-raising is an essentially moral act',[8] once conception and its continuation or otherwise has been dealt with, children rarely feature in ethical thinking until they are old enough to contemplate sex before marriage.

Yet it is important to take an ethical perspective on how children are treated. By way of example, I should like to pursue the question of force-feeding, for it raises questions about how far a parent's responsibility extends, and what level of intervention is appropriate. We recognize that this is an ethical issue when it relates to force-feeding hunger-strikers, or frail elderly people, but if parents do it to small children, it seems unimportant. Yet the battle parents wage against their small children with regard to eating is common, and often quite serious. Children may be held down and have food shovelled into them. They may be made to sit at a table for literally hours till they have eaten whatever it is; they may have the same portion served at every meal until it is eaten; they may be smacked or beaten for refusing to eat. I have heard clergy describe severe punishments given to their small children for not eating – one spoke of this as a matter of spiritual importance, that the child should learn for the good of its soul who was boss. But whether it is a matter of policy, or just a response to frustration, most parents probably get involved in scenarios of that sort at some point or other.

Complex emotions and motivations are involved here. Our relationship with food, and the meaning women especially attach to providing food, go very deep. Sally Cline's book *Just Desserts*[9] is an interesting, if rather anecdotal, study of this. There are probably class differences on this issue as well, with it tending to be the middle-class mothers who worry most about additives and healthy eating – partly because acting on those concerns often involves extra cost. But looked at objectively, what is the justification for forcing a small child to eat? Unless they are sick or have a particular disability, they are not likely to let themselves starve. An exception to this might be where the issue of feeding has been allowed to become such a battle that the child will not eat, and can fail to thrive. This situation is likely to need professional help. It is said that given the choice over a period of weeks, small children select a balanced diet, though this clearly wears off as they get older! Parents may insist that children eat foods which they hate, with the idea that it teaches them to eat a wide range of foods and to be polite. Whether it does work like that is not clear. William Countryman's book *Dirt, Greed and Sex* raises questions about what is acceptable as food, and how some foods become taboo.[10] So if *we* recoil at the idea of eating slugs, should we be forcing our children to eat spinach because it's good for them? How far should individual tastes take precedence over the interests of the cook? Families with older children are more likely to let individuals get what they want to eat, so this tension is less in evidence.

From birth, most babies experience hunger and fullness, and changes in appetite. Loss of appetite may be a sign that something is wrong. People can have problems over food later in life because they have been left unable to listen to the signals of their own bodies telling them whether they are hungry or not. If food is used in a power struggle early in our lives, not only can it lead to eating disorders later on, but it can damage the relationship between parent and child. Eating or not eating becomes one of the few ways in which a small child can exercise its own power and assert its individuality – toilet training is another example. These two areas are the focus for battles, in the way that, in an earlier era, control of masturbation was seen as paramount, and led to desperate remedies.

Force as a means of control

One problem with using force[11] as a means of control is that it is of limited use. Though parents might say they cease to use force once the child is mature enough to make its own decisions, actually the cut-off point comes when the child is big enough to resist physical coercion. This may be more of a problem for small mothers than for six-foot fathers, and it is one reason why some parents effectively give up control once their children get bigger. They are lost because they have not developed other means of control which are more appropriate with older children. The child says 'go on, make me', and the parent realizes they can't. Indeed, they have probably sown the seeds of an almighty rebellion. Using force can ensure that a child does what the parent wants. There are instances where this is necessary, because danger threatens, or because there is no time to stop and explain things. This is true with adults as well, if they are about to step in front of a car; but there are questions about its use as a normal means of control, and at what age it should be stopped.

Related to this is the use of superior intelligence or wit to humiliate and control. Many of us will have experienced teachers who were specialists at this kind of thing, and it is very easy to do. However, is it ever right to treat someone like that, and again, what age should it stop? We are likely to disapprove of managers who humiliate their subordinates in that way, but may think the same behaviour does not matter if the recipient is a child. How far should parents rely on their superior strength and power of argument to control their children, rather than trying to use reason and encourage respect? If a parent is only behaving in a certain way because they are powerful enough to get away with it, does that make it right? There is an echo here with the development of the 'just war' theory; which claims that military intervention is right so long as there is a likelihood of victory.[12]

Something also needs to be said here about the psychology of being forced. There are circumstances in which we are forced to do things for which, looking back, we are grateful – like cleaning our teeth or going to school, perhaps. It is an argument parents will often use: 'You'll be grateful to me one day, my girl.' In other circumstances, though, being forced against your will by someone who is much more powerful than you can feel like annihilation. The victim of an assault feels this to an extreme, but it can also be felt in seemingly less severe circumstances. A child who is forced to do something may feel their very identity is being threatened: what they want does not count, so they must be merely an extension of their parents' wishes. *The Mother's Almanac* suggests that when a child rebels, 'it's almost never over the matter at hand but over a piece of power that might be lost. . . . rebellion is born of fear – the fear that someone is blocking his path, taking away his right to grow.' This is not entirely true, since, as I observed earlier, some rebellion may simply be a testing of the waters, rather than a reaction to a threat.

The Mother's Almanac advises that parents shouldn't say 'always', 'never', or 'must', since 'Absolutes beg for an argument.'[13] Counsellors often make the same suggestion to couples who argue a lot. Presumably the exception for parents is on matters of safety, although they might need to watch how they communicate such rules if they are dealing with a child in a rebellious mood. Some problems with teenagers arise from parents insisting on rigid or inappropriate rules. Children generally survive occasional instances of feeling overpowered, but a child who is constantly dominated by their parents is left with scars. Feelings about this may re-emerge in adulthood when people are confronted by bullying, which leaves them with a similar sense of powerlessness.

Children who constantly feel humiliated and of no account will be left with low self-esteem, and anger, which they may direct outwards or inwards. Those who direct it outwards will want revenge; they are the creatures from whom bullies are made. Persistently angry, hurt children can tear a family apart, or be highly disruptive in school. Anger directed inwards may lead to self-harm, and a sense of failure. Outward obedience is frequently desired by parents, but as Anderson and Guernsey say, 'Parenting must never mistake obedience itself as a positive way of producing responsibility . . . Obedience that does not flow from a positive relation of love . . . can only be achieved through the imposition of force and will ordinarily produce hate rather than love.'[14] Controlling children through superior strength or fear is not respecting them, enabling them to grow, or modelling a helpful view of God.

The rights of children

A key question in all this is whether we believe that children have any autonomy, and to what extent we think they have the right of self-determination. Traditionally, children have been excluded from being considered autonomous. Kant, for example, excludes children along with the mentally insane from his discussion of the principle of respect for persons. J. S. Mill includes only those with mature faculties. There is some talk now of rights for children, although statements like the United Nations Declaration on the rights of children are not so much about legally enforceable rights, as about 'moral, social and political objectives which any human society would seek to pursue, for adults as well as children'.[15] Franklin's book claims children as the last forgotten minority whose rights need advocating: 'indignation is often expressed that women or blacks are treated like children; but not so often that children are treated the way they are'. Yet children too are denied political rights, economically disadvantaged, and subject to parents and teachers for punishment and control.[16]

The Children Act does give recognition to the wishes and feelings of children (considered in the light of their age and understanding). The idea that children have the right to be listened to, and to have their views respected and taken account of, is found in the philosophies of many organizations working with children. The Church has not been at the forefront in creating this approach to children, but it has been influenced by it. There does seem to have been a shift towards seeing children as being important in themselves, rather than as 'the Church of the future', or an extension of their parents. This is evident in the Church of England reports *Children in the Way* and *All God's Children*, for example.[17]

The tension between self-fulfilment and the need to live in community with others is one which runs through this book. We have come to value personal happiness as the main aim in life, and those whose happiness has not in the past been considered important have benefited from this. Individualism has its faults as a creed, but it has encouraged us to regard children as real little people in their own right, rather than assuming their thoughts and feelings do not matter, and that they can be treated just as adults like. More knowledge of children's emotional needs has also brought many improvements in the way they are treated. For example, hospitals are today much more ready to involve parents with their children's care, rather than shutting them out and leaving children feeling abandoned. The downside of stressing individual needs has been that children can regard themselves as important without there being any implications for other people. This is especially true where children and young people have their own fast-moving cultures, fed by big business, which sets them apart from adults and community.

Declarations of children's rights assert that children's needs should be viewed in the context of family and community, and met within their families if at all possible. Children's rights only exist over against their families where the family is abusive and no restoration is possible. Clearly, children - like everyone else - will often have to put up with things which are not ideal; and those who are members of a family or community do have to give up some individual autonomy for the sake of the whole group. Where situations are harsh, autonomy may be a luxury which cannot be afforded - and this is the case in many communities across the world. The publicity given to cases of children 'divorcing' their parents conjures up the image of children toting their suitcases around seeking the 'perfect family' where they can do just as they wish. It causes fear in parents, for they know how fallible they are. Suppose they were to be judged on the basis of the worst times of parenting, when their toddler drives them up the wall, or their adolescent challenges all they stand for? The intention of the law in giving children legal rights is that they should be able to escape where their relationship with their parent/s has irretrievably broken down, and they are being damaged by remaining, and this is important. The child 'divorce' has to be seen as a last and desperate measure. It serves no one's interests to break up families which, though fallible, are survivable. Help in repairing damaged relationships offers more long-term security than moving children on whenever relationships get into trouble.

Paternalism

The trouble is that intervention from outside into family life is too often motivated by paternalism.[18] The idea of paternalism gets applied to a state which supplies the needs or regulates the life of a nation or community, and it can be applied to other organizations too. It is based on a nineteenth-century concept of the father who is firm, but whose intentions are assumed to be loving and in the child's best interests. Such a father makes the decisions about the child, even if the child disagrees. This may involve deception, or the non-disclosure of information, but this is acceptable, since the child's best interests are at stake.

Adults act in a paternalistic way when they try to protect children from knowledge of the 'real world'. This may be necessary in some situations – young children may not be able to cope with knowing in detail what the extremes of human cruelty can do, though as they get older they will begin to learn. Although children are much less protected from such things now that they watch so much television, there is still a tendency for adults to cut them off with 'you're too young to know' in areas where we ourselves are uncomfortable – such as sexuality or even politics. I recall a child who got very upset when her grandparents would not discuss the general election with her, on the grounds that she was too young (at eight) to know about politics. Paternalism thinks it knows best, but does not always see the anxieties which develop when the other feels the truth is being concealed from them – this is an issue in medicine, where paternalism is part of the culture. Christian tradition about love of the neighbour is also often paternalistic: it assumes that we know what is best for our neighbour. There has been no recognition of the conflict when the neighbour disagrees – what should the Good Samaritan have done if he was told to 'go away and let me die'?

Paternalism, says Childress, violates the principle of autonomy and respect for persons because it treats them as a child in need of parental control. A strong paternalism will act to improve people's lot whatever they think about it, though this is not helpful for children for the reasons outlined earlier. However, a limited paternalism makes more sense, for it examines whether a person can decide on their own, and overrides them only if it can be shown that they are not competent. Paternalist intervention on a neighbour's behalf, Childress says, is justified if

a) that neighbour has a limitation or a defect and cannot decide properly for themselves;
b) serious harm would result if there was no intervention;
c) there is proportionality – that is, there is more benefit than harm;
d) the least restrictive, least humiliating, and least insulting means of intervention is chosen.

A framework for parental intervention

I would like to suggest that this discussion of limited paternalist intervention provides a framework for parental intervention. Where families were large, and parents working long hours in harsh conditions, there was much less scope for attention to children's every move. In today's families parents and children are more on top of each other, particularly out of school hours and at holiday times. Parents are quick to intervene in their children's lives, though this often takes the form of nagging about irritating but trivial forms of behaviour, and may not tackle behaviour which is more deep-rooted, but ultimately more serious. Parents may be too quick to help younger children out, and not give them enough time to learn, to fail, and to cope with failing – and this may be more true for girls. They may be intrusive in wanting to know all about their children's lives. If, for some children, their parents have little interest in what they do, for others, there is continual interrogation about what they are doing and thinking. It can be a hard lesson for parents to learn that their child's life belongs to the child. Where there is more than one child in the family, some parents intervene frequently, trying to arbitrate between children. Others ignore fighting until it gets on their nerves, then punish severely and often unfairly.

Using Childress's framework to assess what parents are doing may be helpful in looking at some of these issues, though I am not suggesting it is a recipe to be followed in detail:

a) Has a child a limitation, such that they cannot decide properly for themselves? Lack of experience or knowledge is a factor here, and it will still be difficult to judge in some circumstances how much it limits the child. Is a fifteen-year-old competent to decide whether to go on the pill, or to drink in a pub – and what difference does the law relating to alcohol or sexual consent make? In the case of feeding young children, generally they can decide for themselves whether they are hungry, unless their eating patterns have already become seriously disordered. Where children are fighting, in very many cases they are quite capable of sorting it out for themselves. *How To Stop Your Children Fighting*[19] shows how children can be remarkably good at solving arguments when given joint responsibility for sorting things out, and this works better than having a parent tell them what to do. Some schools use a similar approach by getting pupils involved in matters such as tackling bullying. There can be a much better chance of a policy working if pupils feel responsible for it, rather than feeling that it has been imposed on them.

b) Is serious harm likely to result? Many of the areas where parents intervene and get into battles with children could safely be left to work themselves out. Children's eating fads are often in this category. In the case of glue-sniffing or promiscuity, long-term harm can be done. Where children are fighting or arguing, there are occasions where serious harm might result, but most injuries to person, property, or feelings are minor. A common reason for parents intervening is to protect a younger child, and care needs to be taken that one child is not being systematically victimized. Yet it is often difficult to determine who is victim and who the aggressor – there are many things a younger child can do to provoke the older.

c) However, parents are still left having to decide whether the benefit of intervening outweighs the harm. With feeding, the benefit of a child having a daily balanced diet needs to be set against the harm done to the parent-child relationship through a prolonged power struggle, and the long-term consequences of having no control over your own hunger. In serious matters like drug use, actions such as bringing in the police, or making an issue of something, may result in the behaviour getting worse, or in the child running away from home. There is some evidence that if a parent intervenes in conflict between children, quarrels tend to be more frequent, and the children look to the parent to sort things out rather than learning the important lesson of how to solve their own conflicts fairly. Often, the parent does not know the background to the quarrel, and makes the wrong decisions.

d) Finally, what is the least restrictive, least humiliating, and least insulting way to intervene? There will be many times when parental intervention is justified, but doing it in a sensitive way gives it more chance of success. The use of force over feeding fails on these grounds, even if it survives the other conditions. Persuasion, sanctions, or rewards can be useful, though they will not always help a child to learn to assess their own needs or to learn self-discipline. Stepping in where children are fighting may involve no more than separating the warring factions, and letting them sort it out when they're calmer.

The 'just smack'?

One of the big debates still going on around childrearing is the question of whether physical punishment is appropriate – and even whether it should be made an offence for parents to strike their children. This raises interesting questions about how far morality or ideals can be legislated for, particularly in what is perceived as the private realm. For example, should childminders be allowed to smack children in their charge, if that is what the parents wish? One mother who wanted her childminder to be able to smack her son, fought her local council through the courts on this issue during 1993 and 1994, with rulings being overturned as each side lodged further appeals. Yet legislation on this, even if it seems silly in some individual circumstances, is designed to protect children in general from adult carers who might abuse them. High standards have to be set.

Yet in their own homes, very few children have never received physical punishment. In some cases, children are severely abused by their parents, but much more frequent is cuffing, slapping, or beating which is not severe enough to come to the attention of the authorities. Some writers say that resorting to physical punishment always means failure, and perhaps so, but failure is part and parcel of parenting. It has not been shown that the occasional light smack in an otherwise loving home causes any long-term problems. Generalization about physical punishment is in any case difficult. What matters is what punishment works for that particular parent and child, and is appropriate for that misbehaviour. Physical punishment may be acceptable to some children, who prefer it to lectures or sanctions, but totally wrong for another, who will feel utterly humiliated.

All kinds of parents smack, though they vary in how they regard it. Those who believe in guiding children gently may lose their tempers, smack, and feel guilty. Some parents who try to be 'respectful' of their children smack small children when there seems to be no other way to get the message across. Other parents just do it automatically without thinking – and their children sometimes seem not to notice either. Authoritarian parents are likely to regard physical punishment as necessary for discipline, and perhaps even a duty laid on them by God. Support for physical punishment often goes with a Christian commitment. For writers like Dobson, physical punishment is not only sometimes acceptable, but a biblical way for parents to treat their children. He suggests that inflicting minor physical pain enables the parent to control without nagging, and he teaches a painful muscle squeeze which can be used. Parents should react to anything which is a direct challenge to their authority, he says, since, 'Developing respect for parents is the critical factor in child management', and forms the basis for attitudes to other sorts of authority. Spanking for deliberate flouting of the parents' authority should happen from eighteen months to ten years old – though most should stop by the age of six.

Dobson claims that the disciplinary event provides an excellent opportunity for good communication and the expression of love, when the child goes weeping to the parents' arms.[20] He refers to Proverbs 23. 13-14: 'Don't hesitate to discipline children. A good spanking won't kill them. As a matter of fact it may save their lives.' Though some dispute the biblical texts about punishment, arguing that 'the rod' is like a shepherd's rod which guides and protects, the Bible clearly does make reference to the beneficial nature of physical punishment, and it would have been widely practised. The question is whether we are bound by the practices of that time. Children were in any case regarded differently in biblical times. Childhood was a different experience, and children were expected to play a part in the adult world much earlier than they are today. Though Jesus himself does hold that children have a place in the Kingdom of God, and embraces and welcomes them, they are not at the centre of his message, and neither does he teach them directly. The principle, says Barton, is that Jesus is encountered and helped when the child who is the least of all humans is helped, and this must be the principle we take forward today.[21]

Dobson does believe that such punishment should be rare and limited, but it is easy for this to become the main way in which parents try to control their children, so that punitiveness becomes a central part of the parent-child relationship. In the wider field, many people, and especially men, still push for corporal punishment in institutions, and for young offenders. Spock comments that the view that 'you either punish a child physically or you bring up a spoiled one is fairly common, held oftenest by males and most especially by childless people'.[22] A recent Home-School association meeting at my children's primary school on the subject of 'Discipline' had an attendance of forty, mainly men, in contrast to the normal attendance of a dozen, mainly women. Physical punishment is advocated both in the home and in the cries to bring back flogging for joyriders or vandals. Because we live in a culture which frequently portrays violence as the only solution to wrong-doing, and which yearns for quick and easy action, it is hard to challenge this. Yet as Ronald Preston points out in his piece on this in the *New Dictionary of Christian Ethics*, there is no evidence that flogging has any effect on reducing crime. It only offers reform in those in whom it is least needed, and who could have reformed through other means anyway. He is right to suggest that the root question is, 'What is it in human nature that leads so many to be firmly in favour of corporal punishment?', and to ignore the evidence that it isn't helpful.

The longing for easy solutions

One element in this is that our culture values control very highly. Schaef makes much of this in her analysis of contemporary culture in the United States, and describes how God is made into the supreme controller, 'white, male, and in charge'. Schaef observes, 'The God of the Addictive System, who is the God that religion teaches and who in truth has little in common with the God of the Old and New Testaments, is God the Controller. It follows, then, that if it is possible to be God as defined by that system, one must try to control everything, and we do!'[23] I have already noted this desire for easy answers, certainty about what we are doing. The more we lack self-confidence, the more likely we are to be attracted by simple solutions – and force is the simplest solution there is. If someone strikes you, strike them back. If someone does wrong, beat them and they won't do it again. These have always been popular philosophies, and their appeal is still widespread. We are seeing the rise of vigilante groups, dealing out swift justice to wrongdoers in their neighbourhoods – and three-quarters of the population approve of such action, according to one survey. Complicated questions about making sure the right person has been punished, the appropriate level of punishment for a particular offence, and asking why offenders act as they do, and therefore how best they can be stopped, do not enter the picture.

On the international scene, there are repeated calls for force to be used to end conflicts – the Gulf War was a simple matter of 'giving a bully a good hiding', intervention in former Yugoslavia was simply a matter of bombing the aggressor . . . only at this point the argument fell apart. There was no old-fashioned, military solution, where three sides slaughtered each other; and where not the aggressor but the civilian population was most likely to suffer. There was no easy 'new world order' political solution, when such violence and loathing existed. Terrible things happen, locally and internationally, and, despite all our centuries of sophistication, there is no easy answer.

The parallel between the domestic and the international can be overdone, but is thought-provoking. Faber and Mazlish reflect that listening to the news is like listening to parents' stories about sibling relationships:

> disputes over territory, disputes over belief systems; the 'have-nots' jealous of the 'haves'; the big guys muscling in on the little guys; the little guys bringing their complaints to the UN and the World Court; long, complicated histories of bitterness and distrust being played out with invective and bombs.[24]

How we learn to deal with such disputes at the domestic level may influence how we tackle the much more complicated situation which exists at national and international levels, if it is a question of values as much as practical expediency. There is some evidence that a real will to forgive and to find reconciliation can sometimes bring change at that wider level. Brian Frost documents some examples in *The Politics of Peace*.[25]

Believing that some change is possible, though there are no complete solutions, is essential here. As Sharon Welch observes, it is very easy for the middle classes, who expect to be able to make things work, to be tempted by cynicism and despair when things go wrong: 'Becoming so easily discouraged is the privilege of those accustomed to too much power, accustomed to having needs met without negotiation and work, accustomed to having a political and economic system that responds to their needs.' For many others in the world, there has never been a guarantee of success. We need, says Welch, an ethic of risk which 'begins with the recognition that we cannot guarantee decisive changes in the near future or even in our lifetime', but this does not mean ceasing to struggle, and to imagine a different world. Things should not be judged by immediate results, but by the possibilities which are created: 'Responsible action means changing what can be altered in the present even though a problem is not completely resolved. Responsible action provides partial resolutions to the inspiration and conditions for further partial resolutions by others.'[26]

The limits of intervention

All of this is relevant for families, for here too neither control by force nor peaceful, purely democratic methods are solutions to the way children behave. When children are small they can be controlled by extreme methods, but they cannot be made perfect. Severe methods will leave permanent distortion in the child's personality. Society today needs people who are creative, entrepreneurial, and flexible: cowing children into obedience and submission cannot produce that. It also needs people who are altruistic, who recognize that other people matter. This cannot simply be taught; it must be modelled. Our recognition that children are unique individuals, have feelings, must be respected, means we cannot resort to solutions which are purely punitive and deny that children matter. This is why it is always easier to make general comments about how other people's children should be subject to harsh physical control, whilst being reluctant to use these methods on one's own children. Plenty of parents do close down their emotions and treat their children harshly, but it is much less easy to do this because living with children makes parents aware of their children's individuality, and the need for flexibility in dealing with them.

At the same time, society cannot afford to let people's worst elements of greed, violence, and selfish individualism run riot. There must be control, and limits set on what kind of behaviour is permissible. Raising children is not an entirely democratic affair, and appeals to reason will not always bring harmony. This is partly because childrearing is about socialization of children into the habits and norms of a society. Parents have a duty to instruct their children in this if they are to make their way in the world – an adult in our society who eats yoghurt with their fingers, or who goes around with their hand down their trousers, will generally encounter problems in the world!

The democracy which belongs in family life is not one which allows everybody's contribution to carry equal weight: parents do have the ultimate responsibility. Also, it is important for children to learn to adapt to the wishes of others. But parents need constantly to have the future in mind – if the aim is for offspring to become independent, then they need to be able to contribute and take responsibility gradually as they get older. The whole point of discipline is to enable this to happen. Parents do not need to focus on punishment of misbehaviour in order to provide effective discipline. The emphasis has to be on '"steering" the child through the shallows and rapids of life, by example and with the encouragement that fosters growth and development'.[27] Anderson and Guernsey refer to Paul's teaching that parents should raise children in the discipline and instruction of the Lord (Eph. 6. 1–4). Their understanding of discipline is also about 'steering' – controlling direction as a gardener does by pruning plants, or harnessing energy as a rider guides a horse. Instruction means to place something in the mind, rather than telling children what they must and must not do. Children's responsibility is to obey parents, but Anderson and Guernsey stress the fact the word 'obey' is rooted in the verb to listen.

This has implications for the instruction of children in faith. Some Christians speak approvingly of indoctrination, as Dobson does, saying it should happen at a young age, and will then stay with them for good. They should be taught ultimate loyalty to God, and that defying God's moral laws leads to certain consequences – sickness and death. Dobson seems to believe that wrong-doing and suffering and good behaviour and rewards go together naturally. Yet real life does not bear this out, and the Bible itself shows God's people coming to realize that this is not the case. There is no guaranteed way to turn children into Christian adults. It may be possible to frighten them into being conforming adults, but faith will only grow to maturity if it has been freely embraced. The Kitzingers' fascinating book *Talking with Children About Things That Matter*[28] has a section on religion which suggests that banning children from having anything to do with religion is the surest way to get them interested! This is not being seriously advocated here, but should warn us against thinking there is a secret which solves all problems.

Anderson and Guernsey refer to a survey looking at levels of control and support for adolescents, and what effect this had on them. They conclude that what matters most is not the degree of control to which children are subjected, but how much support they get:

> children of supportive parents who care about them and who have the ability to communicate that care so that the child feels loved are likely to experience a better sense of self-worth, to associate better with others in the community, and to be less likely to get involved with the destructive lifestyles of the counterculture.[29]

This conclusion is borne out for our society by *Crime and the Family*, where the level of supervision and care by parents is seen to be the most significant factor in influencing how children turn out. Children and young people clearly need to be valued and supported with appropriate levels of control. Making control the prime value does not lead to children feeling valued. But children who know themselves to be loved are able to see that parental limit-setting is an expression of love rather than a desire to dictate their lives paternalistically.

Notes

1. Quoted in R. Anderson and D. Guernsey, *On Being Family* (Michigan, William B. Eerdmans, 1985), p. 119.

2. Quoted in R. Gill, *Moral Communities* (Exeter, University of Exeter Press, 1992), p. 37.

3. Quoted in L. De Mause, ed., *The History of Childhood* (New York, Harper & Row, 1975), p. 214.

4. B. Hoggett, 'The Children Bill: The Aim', *Family Law* 1989, p. 217.

5. Quoted in A. Phoenix, A. Woollett, and E. Lloyd, eds, *Motherhood* (London, Sage, 1991), p. 19.

6. C. Lee, *Friday's Child* (Wellingborough, Thorsons, 1988), p. 40.

7. *Heart of the Matter* BBC TV, 19 July 1992. This father was speaking of a decision to refuse an operation for a baby with a heart defect, which was very unlikely to have helped.

8. R. Bondi, writing in J. Macquarrie and J. Childress, eds, *A New Dictionary of Christian Ethics* (London, SCM Press, 1986), p. 85.

9. S. Cline, *Just Desserts* (London, André Deutsch, 1990).

10. W. Countryman, *Dirt, Greed and Sex* (London, SCM Press, 1990).

11. I use the word to indicate superior strength and restraint, not physical violence, though it can lead on to that.

12. Contributions from theologians during the period of the Gulf War asserted this, though it is not part of the earliest theory and is actually rather dubious ethically. I am grateful to my Oxford Ministry Course students for pointing this out.

13. M. Kelly, *The Mother's Almanac* (New York, Doubleday, 1989), pp. 115 and 110.

14. Anderson and Guernsey, *On Being Family*, p. 123.

15. B. Franklin, *The Rights of Children* (Oxford, Basil Blackwell, 1986), p. 14.

16. M. Hoyles, quoted in Franklin, *The Rights of Children*, p. 2. Franklin's book makes some interesting points, though such works tend to be insufficiently rooted in the real experience of children and parents. See also D. Archard, *Children: Rights and Childhood* (London, Routledge, 1993) for a critique of ideas about children's rights.

17. National Society/Church House Publishing, *Children in the Way*, 1988, and *All God's Children*, 1991.

18. The description I use comes from James Childress's piece in Macquarrie and Childress, *A New Dictionary of Christian Ethics*.

19. A. Faber and E. Mazlish, *How to Stop Your Children Fighting* (London, Sidgwick and Jackson, 1989).

20. J. Dobson, *The New Dare to Discipline* (Eastbourne, Kingsway, 1993), pp. 20 and 31.

21. S. Barton, entry on 'Children' in J. Green and S. McKnight, eds, *Dictionary of Jesus and the Gospels* (Downers Grove, IVP, 1992).

22. B. Spock, *Parenting* (London, Michael Joseph, 1989), p. 144.

23. A. Schaef, *When Society Becomes an Addict* (San Francisco, Harper & Row, 1988), p. 47.

24. Faber and Mazlish, *How to Stop Your Children Fighting*, p. 207.

25. B. Frost, *The Politics of Peace* (London, Darton, Longman & Todd, 1991).

26. S. Welch, *A Feminist Ethic of Risk* (Minneapolis, Fortress Press, 1990), pp. 7, 15 and 20.

27. M. Herbert, *Discipline* (Oxford, Basil Blackwell, 1989), p. 11.

28. S. and C. Kitzinger, *Talking with Children About Things That Matter* (London, Pandora Press, 1989).

29. Anderson and Guernsey, *On Being Family,* p. 136.

chapter ten

Can Parents Be Forgiven?

what of yesterday when she chased the baby in my room
*   and I screamed*
OUT OUT GET OUT & she ran
right out but the baby stayed,
unafraid. what is it like to have
a child afraid of you. your own
child, your first child, the one
youre expected to be most nervous with, the one no one
                                                    expects
you to be perfect with (except women in parking lots),
the one who must forgive you if either of you are to survive.
                                                    <u>*Alta*</u>[1]

When the earth receives the parents, the children receive
their freedom.
                                                    <u>*Russian folk saying*</u>[2]

Look at your family, past or present, with a tolerant
attitude. On some level, we are all wounded creatures
struggling to satisfy essential needs.
                                                    <u>*Patricia Love*</u>[3]

Parents who expect their children to be perfect produce
children who expect their parents to have been perfect.
                                                    <u>*Jan Payne*</u>

Can parents be forgiven? The answer clearly depends on what
they've done. One of the few certain things in this world is that

we have all had parents, whether we knew both or either of them or not, and that they have left a legacy in our lives through their presence or absence. That legacy may be good, so that no forgiveness is necessary. It may be utterly destructive, so that we have not reached, and may never reach, the point where forgiveness is even possible. Some of us will have lost touch with the child we once were, forgetting or blocking out the experiences we had, for good or ill. But we have all been shaped by our childhood experiences and our parents' influence; the way we behave now in our relationships to authority, to those we love, to God, will reflect our upbringing. When I talk of children and parents here, I am generally speaking of those who take on parental roles, whether they are the natural mother or father or another adult. Unless those who took on these roles for us have come and gone very quickly, they are likely to have left a mark on our lives somewhere. There can be particular difficulties where step-parents have come into a child's life later on, but much of what is said in this chapter still applies.

The legacy of childhood

When we hear the stories of the damage parents have done, or reflect on any destructiveness which happened in our own upbringing, it can be easy to write families off altogether. Yet few of those who focus on the negative side of family life suggest that the parenting function should in general be taken over by the state or the community. The recognition that some families are damaging should lead to helping them to do their task more effectively, not to their dismantling. This seems to be the stance taken by many who have suffered, or are suffering, abuse as children. Their dream is usually that the abuse will stop and good relationships come about, rather than that they should be taken away from their families.

Many adults spend the middle parts of their lives coming to terms with what happened to them as children. We hear much about survivors of abuse dealing with newly surfaced memories – perhaps triggered by becoming parents themselves, or by hearing others talk. A social worker in a hospital commented how often pregnancy can bring such memories to the surface for women who have been abused as children. Even for those adults who have not suffered abuse, though, mid-life is often a time for re-examining their relationship with their parents. Parents age and die, and people who become parents begin to see their parents in their own behaviour in new ways. These feelings about parents may or may not be articulated, but general observation shows that reorienting ourselves towards our parents is a common experience in mid-life.

Those who want to go into more depth have plenty of opportunities nowadays: therapy may be too expensive to consider (though it is sometimes available free or cheaply for those in great need), but there are numerous self-help manuals available from bookshops: 'The hurtful legacy of toxic parents manifests itself in adulthood as difficulties with relationships, careers, decision making, and depression', says the blurb on one book. 'Whatever the burden you carry . . . Dr. Forward can help release you from the demons of self-blame once and for all.'[4] There is also a growing amount of Christian material which lets you do the same thing, but uses Christian language instead: 'Whatever the burden you carry, Jesus can release you once and for all.' What makes this material curious is that most of us will eventually be parents ourselves, or have some sort of contact with children; yet that aspect is put into a separate category from the one in which we are, as it were, victims of our parents. The assumption seems to be that *we* can never screw things up as badly as our parents did, ignoring the fact that they probably started out with just the same kind of optimism we have.

Once again, as with books on childrearing, there seems to be a fundamental divide between Christian and secular literature. The former emphasizes forgiveness of parents, the latter may very strongly denounce forgiveness as destructive to the person's development. One thing which may make a difference is the extent of the damage parents have done. Some things can be cleared up by talking over what happened in childhood, and understanding can lead to forgiveness; but in many other cases, things are more complex than this. Popular Christian literature on the family can find it hard to address the painful, destructive aspects of family life, for this seems to threaten the notion of the family as a divinely ordained building block for society. This would be true of Ortlund's work, where serious violence and abuse do not seem to be possibilities, at least in Christian homes. At one point she comments: 'Commitment means a willingness to sometimes be unhappy. Remember what the angel of the Lord told Hagar when she ran away from home? "Return . . . and submit" [Gen. 16.9].'[5] However, the main focus of this chapter is not on the extremes of destructive parental behaviour, the sort of abuses that result in criminal prosecution if uncovered. I have written about this in *Distorted Images*, and such behaviour, and the trauma which results from it, need very careful handling. The emphasis here is on parental behaviour which is seen as normal and acceptable, but which none the less leaves scars. The extremes of abuse are of course related to this, but, as I have indicated, will not be my main focus here.

Discovering who we are

One of the tasks teenagers and young adults face is to carve out their own identity over against the expectations and ideas their parents have of them. The struggle to be your own person may take many years to resolve, and middle-aged people may still be caught up in it. There is a question here as to how much we are formed by our parents, and how much we are born as very different, unique individuals. The idea of children as 'wet cement' implies that they can be formed by their parents' behaviour, and yet parents know that children come into the world with different personalities. If we look back on our early lives, we can usually recognize our *selves* with all our autonomy and uniqueness. Yet at the same time, we can be conscious that our parents influenced and formed us, through their attitudes towards us. Those whose parents had very fixed ideas of what their children should be like can reach adulthood unsure of who they really are.

One problem many people face is that of being labelled as children: the clever one, the musical one, the bad one, the happy one. Being imprisoned by such labels can be devastating, for they do not allow the person to have a range of feelings and abilities. The person labelled happy, for example, may find it impossible to own up to personal difficulties. Something similar may happen with Christians in churches, where they are assumed to be joyful and free of doubt. Faber and Mazlish report some of the difficulties adults experience as a result of being labelled in childhood. Andrew Stanway observes that children need 'to be loved consistently, for themselves alone and not on the condition that they be something special or different from what they really are. This kind of love can withstand even quite bad parenting in other ways because it gives a child a sense of worth and stability that will last a lifetime.'[6]

As I have noted before, if parents believe that children are predominantly bad and must be strictly held down, this will affect children's sense of worth. However, if parents can develop trust in their children, and confidence that their children will manage in life, that enables children to believe in themselves. Similarly, to be loved and trusted as an individual who has value in God's eyes gives a sense of worth and stability – though unfortunately, much Christian language about God's love undermines the sense of human uniqueness and value. People are said to be worth something to God not because there is anything good or of value in them, but because God is the sort of God who loves the lowest of the low. Helen Oppenheimer's stress in her writing on the irreplaceability and lovableness of the human person before God is worth looking at here.[7] Knowing that we are valued gives us a base from which to form equal and interdependent relationships in community, rather than leaving us desperately seeking approval from others, or accepting abuse because we feel it is all we deserve.

Letting go and growing up

Parental love needs to have the hallmarks of trust and confidence in the maturing child, because, as Herbert Anderson points out, it is 'The parental love that lets go and sets children free to serve in the world [which] parallels the love of God in Christ.' Families have to encourage individuation so that people can become autonomous enough to leave home for the sake of the gospel.[8] Yet letting children go is very hard. Many people's experience of parenthood is an acute and painful love for the child which changes in intensity, but lasts in some form for ever. So the urge for parents to protect and make decisions on their children's behalf is very strong. It is hard to stand by and watch someone they love making what seem to be the wrong decisions, whether that person is six, sixteen, or sixty.

It can be difficult for parents to let older children go – to acknowledge that a young person in their twenties, thirties, or even older, is now an adult and is responsible for their own decisions. It is known that parents or partners of addicts often carry on excusing and covering up for them, bailing them out when they are in trouble. Similarly, parents of adult offspring with other difficulties can collude with childish behaviour, when they actually need to force their son or daughter to stand on their own feet. There is a difficult line to tread between love and care for another, and preventing them from taking responsibilities for themselves.

There is a temptation, too, for adult children to expect their parents to continue to look after them in some circumstances, whilst fiercely asserting their independence in other areas. Many a young and not-so-young adult visiting the parental home expects to be waited on hand and foot by their mother, or to have their children looked after because 'Mum won't mind'. When elderly parents become dependent themselves, the role reversal can prove difficult to manage for both parties. Adult children in their turn may become over-protective, something I notice in myself when accompanying my (robust) seventy-six-year-old father on the roller-coaster at the theme park near his home! Other people face decisions about dealing with a frail elderly parent who wishes to live alone, but whose vulnerability causes them concern. Again, it is a difficult line to tread between protecting an older person, and allowing them to continue to enjoy life, and take their own risks.

This tension between protectiveness and risk-taking is evident in Christian life too. We are often reluctant to take risks with our faith – not just in how we live, but in how we think. We may look to others to tell us what we ought to believe, rather than being prepared to think things out in order to make them our own. As I have already noted, we want to deal in absolutes, to know exactly what we ought to be doing. Absolutes do have a place, yet merely demanding obedience to a set of rules leaves people without any capacity for real moral thinking. They may survive whilst they are given the answers from above, but be unable to find any way forward when faced with the messy complexity of moral choice in real life. While it may be no bad thing to be obedient to the values set out in the Christian gospel, the mindset of obedience easily leads people to follow anyone who is strong, without being critical of *what* they are being asked to do. It seems that people are only happy to be God's children if they can remain for ever under the age of consent and responsibility – leaving it all in the hands of their heavenly father. This has its place at some stages in the spiritual journey, as Fowler shows,[9] but we need to move on from that to discover what it means to be an *adult* child of God.

Some have criticized the idea of God as Father for keeping believers in a state of spiritual infancy. Yet this comment says more about our beliefs about the parent or father/child relationship than about God. A good parent allows their children to come to maturity and reach their own decisions; stands by them when in trouble, welcomes them when they come home, and rejoices when children become mature people with their own place in the community. Christians are to move from the milk suitable for infants on to solid food, to put away childish things, to work out their own salvation with fear and trembling for God is at work in them. Christian life is a journey, a pilgrimage, not perpetual infancy. Whether we start with what we know to be good parenting, or with what we know of God's relationship with us, the message that God's Fatherhood or Motherhood allows us to grow up is the same. Just as we may think we know all there is to know when we are young adults, so Christians who have grown in their faith may feel confident that they know just what God is like. Without realizing it, they may define and try to control God through their pronouncements. God accepts this vulnerability, looking, as parents look, for their offspring to come to a more mature wisdom which realizes how little it knows and understands.

We can also extend this to include the way that adult children end up taking care of frail elderly parents. The child/parent image is not simply a paternalistic one, but involves interdependence. If Christ is served when we care for others in need, here too God is made vulnerable, reliant – as in the incarnation – on human care. 'Family' metaphors of humankind's relationship with God easily become limited to seeing ourselves as children and God as

Almighty Father – or even Mother. But family imagery can be much wider and richer than this. We are also Christ's sisters, brothers, mothers, and friends (Matt. 12. 48-50). There are of course limits to how far we can use the metaphor of God as Parent, and it will always be an incomplete image. As McFague points out, metaphor always carries within it the whisper 'it is and it is not'.[10] Yet it is worth keeping room for it, because it makes ordinary domestic relationships a springboard for understanding something of who God is, and what we can be.

Parental imperfections

But what if parents treat children harshly, so that the only God they can imagine is judgemental or distant, or demands too high a standard? I have already discussed the harmful effects both of over-strict discipline and failure to set limits. These problems usually centre around the child's will – whether it is broken, or whether the child rebels, or whether she or he is uncontrolled. Yet there are also problems for children who do not rebel, but are instead the epitome of Christian children, 'mild, obedient, good as He'. The difficulties caused for 'good' children in families is explored by Patricia Love in *The Chosen Child Syndrome*. Children who are marked out as 'good' within a family may feel that they are in effect being told they are not to have problems or needs: 'at least you never cause us any worry' conveys the message 'you cannot have any problems'. Some children are expected to take care of their parents emotionally, and sometimes physically, and may be praised as very good – they may even win 'Children of the Year' awards. Yet they may be left without anyone seeing that they have needs too. I suspect that Christian parents may be more prone to creating this syndrome, since the values being praised are often identified with Christian values of love and self-sacrifice. Telling a child that they are a special child in the family can also make it difficult for that child to be themself, to fail and do wrong occasionally. Such children may feel doomed always to disappoint their parents, because they can never live up to the ideal in their parents' minds – and it does not do much for sibling relations if one child is always being held up as the one who does no wrong.

Some children who are treated in this way have severe problems in adult life. This will particularly be the case where their treatment had no let-up or counter-balancing factors. Probably many others, though marked, have been able to cope; any difficulties caused have not taken over their adult lives. Few of us had entirely happy childhoods: our parents were deficient from time to time, they wounded us as well as nurturing us as best they knew how. But we are all somewhere on a continuum which stretches from good-enough childhoods through to those which were so abusive that they destroyed our capacity to relate in adult life. It is worth noting that such issues can come to a head when elderly parents are cared for by their adult children. Having three generations in a household may be delightful, but it can also bring strain, and it can be very difficult to be caring towards a parent who has damaged or even abused you in your childhood. The mixed feelings which come from doing a full-time caring job can be even more stressful in such cases. What is it like to have someone who cast a shadow over your life now dependent on you for everything? What is it like to be at the mercy of a grown child who dislikes you?

One of the strongest critics of methods of childrearing in recent years has been the psychoanalyst Alice Miller. She writes passionately about the damage inflicted on children by well-meaning parents, 'the unintentional persecution of children by their parents, sanctioned by society and called child-rearing'. She asserts that the Judeo-Christian tradition is incriminated in this: 'Can it be that the coercive measures of "poisonous pedagogy" would have less power over us and our culture if the Judeo-Christian tradition had not lent them strong support?' For it shows loving fathers tormenting sons – Abraham and Isaac, God and Job, God the Father and Jesus. In paradise, humankind is forbidden under threat of loss of love and abandonment to eat of the Tree of Knowledge, to ask questions about the world. 'Thou shalt not be aware', is a commandment which predates the Ten Commandments.[11]

Miller asserts that 'it is not a matter of assigning blame to individual parents, who, after all, are themselves victims of this system, but of identifying a hidden societal structure that determines our lives'. Parents' behaviour can be better understood if it

180

is seen as part of an overall system, and we should not fail to denounce that damaging system simply in order to protect parents. The fact that mothers and fathers may feel guilty and distressed if what they have done is made clear should not stop us trying to move forward. Parents cannot expect to be perfect, and they too are victims of their childhood and childrearing ideology. Adults need to express their rage at being failed, and not feel they must defend mothers from all accusation: 'We cannot undo the harm done to children, neither by blaming nor by defending the parents, but perhaps we can help to prevent future damage if we do not have to deny the truth out of our need to defend ourselves or our parents.'[12]

Many criticisms can be made of Miller's work, but she undoubtedly has some useful insights to set alongside other analyses of what happens to children in families. She does raise acutely the question of how far parents can be blamed for the damage they cause, and whether it is Christian to refuse to blame them for fear of hurting their feelings. How responsible are parents for what they do in relation to their children, if they have done their best? There is much that can be said about the nature of responsibility and blame which I cannot go into here. However, it is worth noting that it is possible for someone to accept responsibility for things for which they are not strictly to blame. Children can be very quick to say 'don't blame me' when one of their actions has caused a plate to break, for example. What they mean is that they did not intend the breakage; though as a matter of fact it was their action which caused it. It is hard enough to apologize for problems arising from weakness and deliberate fault, but perhaps harder still to accept responsibility for what we do through ignorance, particularly if we felt we were acting in the best way possible at the time. Mothers in the 1950s who left their children crying for long periods rather than pick them up and feed them were following what they thought was best for the child. Yet therapists say that many adults today are coping with the traumatic effects of such treatment. In that sort of case, it can help for parents to acknowledge the consequence of their actions, to accept responsibility, and to allow an adult child to express their feelings about what it has done to them.

The trouble is that there are so many things which parents seem to have done wrong: they have not only eaten sour grapes to set their children's teeth on edge, but lemons and unripe gooseberries as well! As more and more trauma is traced back to early childhood, so parents become more and more responsible. Not only what the mother eats during pregnancy, but even her feelings during that time are said to affect what kind of child she has. We are seeing the beginnings of cases where children sue their mothers for taking drugs or smoking during pregnancy. Similarly, there was a case brought recently by a young adult against a local authority for not handling his care properly when he was young. The prospect of suing parents for not bringing you up properly seems to be on the horizon. In Isaiah, the prophet asks: 'Does the pot complain that its maker has no skill? Does anyone dare to say to his parents, "Why did you make me like this?"' (Isa: 45. 9 -10). The answer increasingly seems to be that they do.

The question at issue here is what a child actually has a right to. No one has a right to perfect parenting, for such a thing does not exist. We can expect to be fed, sheltered, and have some loving attention paid to us, but it is difficult to use the language of rights here. We cannot introduce quality control and value for money principles into family life without destroying it. In any case, such an approach takes a child out of the family and community as if they had rights over against it. It may be a misfortune to be born into poverty, or into a nation at war, but we cannot expect to choose the circumstances into which we are born, and neither can being born into a rich family in a peaceful nation be a guarantee of health and happiness. There are too many variables which affect who we are and what happens to us to be able to blame parents entirely. And since our parents can blame their parents and our grandparents can blame their parents, it is impossible to say where the buck stops.

There seems to be little profit in going down the road of 'rights' or of seeking one person to blame. Once we have recognized what happened to us as children, it may be possible to talk it through with our parents, if they are still alive, and to ask them to acknowledge the ways in which what they did affected us. Where parents have died, or are unable to respond for one reason or another, it may be more difficult to come to terms with our childhood. Self-help books offer some suggestions about this, such as writing a letter to the dead parent.

Having some idea of why our parents did what they did does begin to take us forward. We may be able to see the problems they were living with, learn what advice they were given, understand whether they operated from ignorance, weakness, or their own deliberate fault. If we are parents ourselves, we may see how we reproduce the patterns we learnt in our childhood. It is useful to reflect on the things we feel we must never do to our own children, for this points to our own early experience. It is common for parents to hear their own mother's or father's voice when they are criticizing their children. They may consciously try to avoid particular forms of behaviour, yet find themselves doing it all the same. Or they may feel as if their own parent is sitting on their shoulder questioning and criticizing what they are doing: 'You're not going to let her speak to her father like that, are you?' Understanding what is going on can encourage us to challenge the attitudes which are harmful to children generally, so as to encourage more positive ones in the future.

Must children forgive?

Discovering where responsibility lies is one thing, but forgiveness is another. Many Christians make it an essential component of family life. Anderson states that since 'in no other context of human life does our sinfulness show as clearly as it does in the family', forgiveness is an 'essential component of being children and parents together'.[13] Moynagh stresses that whilst children can be critical of their parents, they must acknowledge and thank parents for what they have done, and forgive them. Failure to do this, he says, is a failure to obey the commandment to honour (or 'glorify and exalt' in his interpretation) your parents. Forgiveness breaks hurtful patterns in family life, and is 'perhaps the most effective family therapy there is'.[14] It is one thing to talk about the importance of forgiveness as a necessary currency in everyday family life. Without readiness to forgive misunderstandings and hurts, no relationship can thrive. In ordinary encounters within families, we need more generous forgiveness of one another.

However, it is quite another thing to insist on forgiveness where there has been consistent bad treatment in the home. Moynagh quotes the case of Eric, who

> felt gnawed away inside by resentment towards his mother and father. He sometimes felt like hitting out at other people as a way of getting even with his parents. In counselling he was shown how forgiving his parents so that he could affirm them . . . would reduce his resentment and the tension inside him. He did so, and found new acceptance at home.[15]

The trouble is that things are rarely that simple. Anger and resentment are strong emotions, and trying to forgive without dealing with the anger can lead to further problems in the long run. Christian theology stresses the importance of such things as love, forgiveness, and self-sacrifice, but the vision of the family in which such things are supposed to happen so often fails to connect with the messy reality of most people's experience.

Jim Conway, in *Adult Children of Legal or Emotional Divorce*, also makes forgiveness a central element. He does emphasize that the fact that a real hurt has been done must be recognized, and grieved over. It may include challenging the parent who did the damage, but needs to move on to letting go, refusing to hold a grudge. The parent has not earned forgiveness, but is to be given it freely and permanently. The problem is to be relinquished into God's hands: 'The focus of forgiveness must always be grace. Forgiveness is always unmerited.'[16] The difficulty with those who stress forgiveness is that it all too easily comes across as an oversimplification of the long and painful process of coming to terms with damage.

Therapists tend to be much more scathing about the business of forgiveness. Forgiveness impedes healing, says Forward in a chapter headed 'You Don't Have to Forgive'. Though it is right to give up the need for revenge, we do not have to absolve the guilty party of responsibility if what they were doing was mistreating an innocent child. 'Absolution is another form of denial: "If I forgive you, we can pretend that what happened wasn't so terrible.' Forgiveness is dangerous, says Forward, because it undercuts the ability to let go of pent-up emotions, and people can end up hating themselves even more. The example this counsellor gives is of a devout Christian who had to get in touch with her rage to be healed, and who discovered that God wanted her to get better more than God wanted her to forgive. Forgiveness cannot be forced, and the more severe the hurt, the more time will probably be needed to be angry and to grieve. Forgiveness comes at the end, not the beginning. Parents need to acknowledge what has happened and take responsibility, be prepared to make amends, and to 'earn' forgiveness.[17] Miller too is critical of the idea that a gesture of forgiveness will put everything right. Easy reconciliation by teaching people to forgive and understand their parents is not appropriate unless anger at the damage done has been allowed expression: 'the therapeutic goal of improved inter-action between partners or with other members of the family can be a legitimate one but cannot be compared with the individual's liberation from the results of the harm done to him as a child.'[18]

This is a difficult area for Christians to come to terms with, for we are used to having the virtues of forgiveness thrust at us. It does seem that we have a duty to forgive freely whatever the circumstances. Yet perhaps the knowledge that forgiveness cannot always come easily can help us to rethink what happens when God forgives us. The answer may lie in seeing that forgiveness does not have to mean 'pretending it never happened', but letting go of what has happened. The Greek word translated *forgive* in the Lord's Prayer can have the meaning of letting go, and it is a helpful way of looking at things. Forgiveness in this sense is possible when we have acknowledged what has happened, but can move forward from it, refusing to let it fester in our lives any longer.

Christians are used to confessing their sins at every turn, and receiving forgiveness, but whether we actually accept responsibility is another matter. It is often the case that in human experience, for forgiveness to be complete, the other has to acknowledge what they have done. It can be very annoying to have someone insisting that they forgive us when we are convinced that we have committed no offence. Yet how do we accept responsibility for what we have done as individuals and as community? While it may be easy to feel sorry for deliberate wrong-doing, it is much harder to repent of being wrong simply by virtue of being ourselves. This is an issue men face in dealing with sexism, and white people in dealing with racism. We are not to blame for being formed by the culture in which we grow to maturity, but once we become aware of sexism and racism, we become responsible for repenting of them and doing something about them. It is not a simple matter of confessing one action or thought and receiving absolution, but of constantly challenging those ingrained patterns of thought that we now see to be wrong.

Perhaps it is, as Miller suggests, that we need to repent of the wrong systems of childrearing we are all part of, rather than seeing it only in terms of individual guilt. Christianity does sometimes concentrate on individual guilt to such an extent that corporate wrong is obscured, yet, as Dodd remarks, we must recognize that

> The problem of evil is indeed something which goes beyond questions of individual responsibility, and salvation is more than a device for freeing an individual from his guilt: it must cut at the root of that corporate wrongness which underlies individual transgression. This is, according to Paul, what has actually been effected by the work of Christ. In him [people] are lifted into a new order in which goodness is as powerful and dominant as was sin in the order represented by Adam; or, rather, it is far more powerful and dominant.[19]

Honour one another

The fact that many people feel they ought to forgive their parents does not entirely stem from oppressive religious teaching. It may also reflect an understanding and genuine love for parents which sees them as frail human beings who were scarred in their past, and whom God still loves. When children grow up to become parents themselves, they may learn a new tolerance, seeing that on some level all of us are wounded in some way, and struggling to do our best. Honouring fathers and mothers may mean recognizing them as frail human beings who are not the gods or devils our childish memories make them. We may come to understand why our parents behaved as they did – even if we are critical of it.

It is common for women to find new understandings of their mothers when they go through motherhood themselves. This is often a positive experience, though for some it may bring a fresh realization of the hurts of their childhood. Jean Radford captures some of this when she reflects:

> The desire for motherhood is . . . about . . . the desire to relive my childhood with the mother I desired to have rather than the mother I actually had. Is it that lost child or the lost mother I want to regain? Or both? To go back in fantasy, to recover, to make good, to change things for the better. Dear God, give me the courage to change the things I can change, the serenity to accept the things I cannot, and the wisdom to know the difference. The words of that prayer are the best words I could find, they give a shape and ritual to something in my wish for children. A child is a way of coming to terms with the past?[20]

Adults who are seeking healing for their past have a number of different resources they can turn to. Yet the emphasis is often on taking an assertive stance in relation to parents, and being prepared to cast off ties with parents if the confrontation does not 'work'. They stress the behaviour of the individual in a way which seems to deny the interdependence that exists even in families which have been unhealthy. A false choice seems to be presented here, either inappropriate dependency, or complete independence. Yet we need the sense that we can be related to others, connected in a way that will cause pain as well as joy, without this being a threat to our sense of self. Trying to sort out a complex muddle of family relationships will not be easy because this sense of connectedness is usually still very real. How *do* you face your parents with the hurtful legacy they have left you, when you know it will cause them pain?

The choice offered seems to be between confronting parents and moving to freedom, or remaining silent but imprisoned. Certainly, remaining silent because we believe that family life should never be troubled by conflict is unhelpful. Jesus was not directly talking about conflict in families when he spoke of bringing a sword rather than peace, and of setting children against parents and parents against children; but his words are a reminder that harmony is not always a positive family value. Other interests may demand that we take risks with relationships. Yet there may be different ways of doing this. Perhaps guidelines are needed for moving a little way at a time, given that not everyone is capable of the one bold step. There is a difference between avoiding confrontation in the mistaken belief that parental authority should never be challenged, and moving gently to try to put relationships right with someone you love. It will be much more difficult for adult children to talk with parents where strict parental authority is upheld than in more open homes where parents have been able to admit they were sometimes wrong. It may help to see that the tensions between parents and children is part of a wider set of relationships - working things through with siblings or other relations, or talking to friends of the family, can be helpful in getting other perspectives on why things happened as they did.

There is some chance of breaking painful patterns of family life when parents keep themselves aware of what it is like to be young, and have reconciled themselves to the pains and joys of their childhood. They have to avoid seeing children as 'other', a different race who do not feel or notice things as we do, who are ignorant and innocent of the things that matter. Equally, we have to avoid seeing our parents as 'other'. For they too are people like us, not a different race who do not feel and notice things like we do, who are ignorant and innocent about the things that matter. Perhaps we can understand honouring our parents in this way. Miller, amongst others, has been severely critical of the way the fourth commandment to honour your parents has been used. She uses the phrase: 'fell victim to the Fourth Commandment', and suggests we need a new commandment to 'Honor [sic] your children'.[21]

But 'honouring parents' can be reclaimed in the sense of granting parents understanding and respect as people, rather than worshipping or obeying them. Teenagers and young adults breaking free of their families of origin may fail to give this kind of respect to their parents, but it is something Christians should be urging them to do. It means that though parents' values and behaviour may seem hopelessly out of touch, they are not automatically ridiculed or denied a voice. Indeed, adults in middle age can treat older people in general (not only their own parents) rather dismissively at times – we can easily become 'ageist'. What might it mean really to see elderly people as individuals deserving of respect? Parents can be forgiven more easily when the relation of adult child to parent is not seen in isolation, but as one dimension of the whole network of relationships of family life, with all their pains and possibilities.

Notes

1. From 'Momma: A Start on All the Untold Stories', by Alta, ©
1974 by Times Change Press, Box 1380, Ojai CA 93024.

2. Quoted in L. De Mause, ed., *The History of Childhood* (New
York, Harper & Row, 1975), p. 397.

3. P. Love with J. Robinson, *The Chosen Child Syndrome* (London,
Piatkus, 1991), p. 11.

4. S. Forward (with C. Buck), *Toxic Parents* (London, Bantam
Books, 1990).

5. A. Ortlund, *Disciplines of the Home* (Milton Keynes, Word UK,
1990) p. 25. She does not seem conscious of the irony of using
Abraham's 'mistress' as a role model!

6. A. Stanway, *Preparing for Life* (London, Viking, 1988), p. 134.

7. See H. Oppenheimer, *The Hope of Happiness* (London, SCM
Press, 1983), and my *A Woman's Work* (London, SPCK, 1989).

8. H. Anderson, *The Family and Pastoral Care* (Philadelphia,
Fortress Press, 1984), p. 38.

9. For a useful brief discussion of faith development, see the report
How Faith Grows (London, National Society/Church House
Publishing, 1991).

10. S. McFague, *Metaphorical Theology* (Philadelphia, Fortress
Press, 1982), p. 13.

11. A. Miller, *Thou Shalt Not Be Aware* (London, Pluto Press,
1990), pp. 22 and 94-5.

12. Miller, *Thou Shalt Not Be Aware*, pp. 194-5 and 301.

13. Anderson, *The Family and Pastoral Care*, p. 97.

14. M. Moynagh, *Home to Home* (London, Daybreak, 1990), p. 62.

15. Moynagh, *Home to Home*, p. 152.

16. J. Conway, *Adult Children of Legal or Emotional Divorce* (Eastbourne, Monarch, 1991), p. 205.

17. Forward, *Toxic Parents*, pp. 186ff.

18. Miller, *Thou Shalt Not Be Aware*, p. 200.

19. C. Dodd, *Commentary on the Epistle to the Romans*. I am indebted to Professor J. Rogerson at the University of Sheffield for this quotation. I do not have the complete reference.

20. J. Radford, in K. Gieve, ed., *Balancing Acts* (London, Virago, 1989), p. 137.

21. Miller, *Thou Shalt Not Be Aware*, p. 203.

chapter eleven

Windfallen Fruits

Three themes are signs of God's intention for creation: the tolerance or even celebration of diversity, the adaptability to change, and the commitment to live interdependently in the world.

Herbert Anderson[1]

Entering into deeper, more meaningful and at the same time juster structures of relating is the kind of redemptive spirituality needed for the transformation of the world.

Mary Grey[2]

But the Spirit produces love, joy, peace, patience, kindness, goodness, faithfulness, humility, and self-control.

Gal. 5. 22-23

The more we hear about society being in a deep moral crisis, and about the death of family life, the more easy it is to despair. We look back longingly to some perceived golden age and call for the 'traditional family values' which we think can solve our problems. I have suggested that the values we usually have in mind cluster around discipline, obedience, control, punishment, conformity, sexual morality, and so on. They are values which will maintain order in society, and they have roots in the Christian tradition. At a time of change and fear, when the world is suffering a severe bout of what has been called Pre-Millennial Tension,[3] we are drawn to values which promise to manage disorder. But the Christian vision is not simply of a society which is carefully ordered. It is of one in which humanity is able to flourish and be creative. We look beyond mere rule-keeping and the imposition of punishment to a world in which love of God and of our neighbour as ourselves sets the agenda. We look for a world in which the Spirit of God is active, and where the fruits of the Spirit can be discovered and can nourish us. We are not alone in holding out this vision, for plenty of people want to see more humane values at the centre of social and family life. It may not always be possible to say exactly what is distinctive about the Christian contribution to the debate about family values. We can only say that our faith leads us in a particular direction, and rejoice if others are on the same road. An affirmation of Christian values, if we are not too possessive about them, may be exactly what many people are wanting to hear.

Throughout this book I have pointed to a set of values which are rooted in the New Testament, though not always spelled out for family life, and in this chapter I should like to draw them together. The 'family values' that I want to set out find their closest echoes in Paul's list in Galatians 5 of the fruits of the Spirit, and they both challenge our thinking, and suggest some practical ways forward for both churches and society. They are not the only values possible, but they are ones which are needed at this point in time. They can have their downside, though, for even gospel values can be distorted. However, if we can grasp how they interact with each other and with our lives, they can be important elements of our Christian witness amidst the present uncertainties.

Community: the interdependence of love

Although 'community' is an overworked word, it can still say something vital about the need for interdependence. If words can also be understood by looking at their opposites, then over against 'community' I would want to set 'isolation', rather than individualism. Christianity has always valued the individual soul, and the movements that have stressed the rights of black people, women, or children to be treated justly and with respect are of great importance. The problem is that we have pursued individual rights and interests in isolation from community. We have failed to make it clear that the rights of an individual must always be limited to some extent by the interests of other individuals and of the world as a whole. Furthermore, Christianity teaches that the individual's relationship with God is expressed in relationships with others, all humankind becomes our neighbour. Yet the choice we seem to be offered is either of individual freedom without society or the denial of individual freedom through enforced obedience to the state – and the collapse of communism makes it appear that only the former option will work. Walsh suggests that our society is dominated by 'a cultural and political attitude that stresses individuality, freedom, autonomy, rights, the separation of religion and politics, reason, tolerance, the non-imposition of belief, and progress'. He adds, 'The political rhetoric simply assumes that we all believe in a vision of life which is individualistic not communitarian, concerned with rights not responsibilities, committed to economic growth not the careful stewardship and just distribution of resources, and committed to a liberal ideal of progress rather than normative historical development.'[4]

Christians have to challenge this view, asking how these came to be the only choices available, and by emphasizing that our full humanity is experienced through interdependence. For us, this is also a reflection of the Trinity, the God who is dynamic relationship. Others, including some in politics and of other faiths, can be heard grappling with the same issues. Many feminists have arrived at a similar position, needing to stress women's individual rights, yet recognizing that relationships with others and collective solutions are essential. Some strands of feminism have bought into an ideology of individual rights which denies the responsibility to value and care for others, but there are other strands in which the vision is of community, 'a society that is organized around human needs: a society in which child raising is not dismissed as each woman's individual problem, but in which the nurturance and well-being of all children is a transcendent public priority.'[5] Christian feminism is usually strong in emphasizing the values of community, friendship, and care for the earth and its people – I have made some reference to Rosemary Ruether and Mary Grey, and there are many other feminist theologians who develop similar themes. If mainstream Christianity were less suspicious of it, a Christian feminist perspective could fill out our understanding of family and community values – and this book is one attempt in this direction.

Christians have to maintain that care for the vulnerable in society is of the utmost importance. Societies are judged by their care for those who are strangers, who are sick, in prison, without shelter, and so on. The 'little ones' who have no power, especially children, are a particular responsibility. Self-interest alone may not lead to care for those who are vulnerable. We are seeing this in society at the moment, where schools which desire a good reputation can feel under pressure to get rid of troublesome pupils, or doctors can be reluctant to keep chronically ill patients on their lists because they consume too many resources. Only a society which feels responsibility for all its members, that we are all in some sense neighbours, can have the will to be inclusive. The word 'community' has been used to mean many things, but we have to reclaim the values of interdependence in community if society is to flourish. Indeed, this is the burden of the message being stressed by many religious leaders. Although this has some-times brought condemnation, it is imperative that we continue to assert the importance of community – and to spell out what this means in practice, in relation to the key social and political issues of the day.

The joy of diversity

Diversity here is not the opposite of 'unity', but of uniformity. Large groups sometimes have to manage by treating everybody in the same way, rather than allowing individual choices. But in human society, the presence of diversity ought to be one of the joys of community. St Paul's image of a body with many working parts captures this sense of diversity in unity. The call for Christian family values is often linked with insistence on the nuclear family of once-married parents and their biological children. However, as I have shown, family takes many different forms for different people and at different times of their lives. Christians cannot restrict themselves to valuing only one particular family form. Even for those Christians who oppose families formed after divorce, deliberately chosen single-parenthood, or gay and lesbian couples, there is still a rich variety of family form, to meet different people's needs at different times. People live alone or with friends, extended families with elderly relations living in, non-residential extended families, step-families or one-parent families formed after a former partner has died, foster families, and so on.

To affirm diversity, however, is not the same as saying that 'anything goes'. Relationships between parents and children and between couples need some sort of regulation for purposes of inheritance and maintenance, even leaving aside the question of emotional security. I also find myself wanting to talk about norms in society in the sense of 'what most people do'. The majority of people do seek a pair-bond which they would like to last, and do have a desire to have children. These things may be worked out in different ways in different communities, particularly taking a global perspective, but they do suggest that support for marriage or something similar, and for childrearing in families, will be a priority for a society that wishes to promote the best interests of its population. I am not convinced by the approach which sets out all the different family forms as if it were a matter of choosing between a variety of equal options. Divorce or single parenthood may end up being the best option in individual circumstances, but few in those situations deliberately choose that course. Most wish that their relationships had worked in the first place, rather than seeing the process of divorce, or having a baby as a single mother, as a life-choice to be sought out. Some single women do speak of their right to have their own child, and may seek AID (Artificial Insemination by Donor) or self-insemination in order to achieve their aim. It is difficult to argue against this in a culture which stresses individual rights so strongly, though it may not be in the long-term interests of a child. It appears to be treating children as commodities – but perhaps judgement needs to be suspended until we hear more from, and know more about, children who have grown up in these circumstances.

Diversity in ways of organizing sexual relationships has caused great concern to Christians. This is partly because we tend to be conservative, and unhappy about change. God is un-changing, we reason, and therefore Christian truth must be unchanging. Yet as Oppenheimer wryly comments, 'It is all very well to preach God's unchanging will: but it is odd to ascribe to

God an inflexibility when circumstances change which would be no virtue in human beings.'[6] God must also be seen as dynamic, challenging us afresh as new options open up to us in each generation.

Following Oppenheimer, it can help if we see marriage and family more as human institutions, which can be blessed by God, rather than as entailing particular universal, divine forms which must be followed by everybody. There is no one God-given style of parenting, for example, when different people and communities of necessity manage family life and childrearing in a variety of ways. We know a lot about the values which sustain good family life, and I shall refer to some of these below, but the precise ways in which these values are expressed will have more to do with class, culture, and life-style than with following a particular recipe exactly.

The patterns described in the Bible are varied, adapted for the different cultures in which people lived, and the same is true in our own history. As I have noted, the Church has at times been able to give God's blessing to other patterns, like cohabitation or polygamy, yet has tried to maintain a commitment to the values which should undergird relationships. It is difficult for the Church to state categorically that cohabitation, say, or remarriage after divorce are always sins, and there will no doubt continue to be debate about these. However, it is part of our witness to say that some sexual relationships are sinful. Those in which partners have no commitment to one another, or which are purely transitory, or in which partners are abusive or indifferent to one another's welfare, contradict the fundamental Christian values of faithfulness, hope, and love – and this may happen within marriage as well as outside of it. As Walrond-Skinner points out, 'The longing for faithfulness, hope and love, expressed in committed relationships, is a longing for the essential values that bind us together as human beings, across cultures and generations, across all our individual differences and across all the differences of family pattern and form.'[7]

Many Christians point to the need for a more positive emphasis on marriage as a way of satisfying and structuring human needs for relationship. But as I have argued, unless

Christians can tackle the assumptions about inequality between men and women built into our concepts of marriage, the romantic ideal we put forward will continue to be found wanting.

The peace found in chaos

Chaos is a useful word because of its meanings in the world of physics. These include the notion that a chaotic, irregular system is actually more stable than a regular one, because it can respond to variations. Family life or form which has to be exactly ordered is threatened by any departure from the norm. Flexibility in ways of managing life and family form allow us to respond to changes more creatively.

However, chaos theory reminds us too that there are patterns in what appears as disorder. The candle flame seems to flicker randomly, but is actually following a chaotic pattern which can be described by simple rules. Chaos here is not the opposite of pattern or harmony, but of rigidity. There is a chaotic peace which can support family life, which is about underlying security and reliability amidst turbulence. If we begin with the value of harmony, we are likely to force people into suppressing their angry and discontented feelings in an unhealthy way – and, as I have said, this can be a particular problem in Christian families. Or they will simply feel inadequate because their family life is so disharmonious. But disharmony, or chaos, is an essential ingredient in family life, not the mark of failure.

Relationships in families are often chaotic, in the usual sense of the word, with their muddle of love, jealousy, desire, and hate. Yet it is in the midst of this that Christ meets us. Dominian refers to the Catholic idea of the 'Domestic Church', and though I do not find that title helpful, Dominian's description of it points to the creativity of chaos: 'In the course of our daily life we have our own spirituality as we struggle to relate lovingly to one another; as we struggle to understand one another; as we make umpteen mistakes and we create umpteen hurts; as we reach one another umpteen times in the twenty-four hours; at those moments we encounter Christ in one another.' Within such everyday things, he says, the ordinary becomes extraordinary, and a symbol of

saving grace. The daily encounters with Christ in the midst of
ordinary experience can then be gathered up in formal Sunday
liturgy.[8] I am reminded by this of some words from a hymn I first
encountered in a Catholic church:

> Take all that daily toil
>   plants in our heart's poor soil,
> Take all we start and spoil,
>   each hopeful dream,
> the chances we have missed,
>   the graces we resist,
> Lord, in thy Eucharist,
> take and redeem.[9]

This kind of conflict within families helps to produce growth
– and must of course be distinguished from chronic fighting,
which leaves family members emotionally or physically battered.
The chaos of family relationships arises as people work out both
their difference and their interdependence, and this has implications
for wider society. It warns us against making harmony the
overriding aim, and encourages us to live with difference and
dislike where necessary, rather than ruthlessly trying to suppress
dissent or proclaiming a false unity. I have referred to Welch's
call for an ethic of risk in society, which can live with the fact that
disagreements cannot be solved and that progress is slow. For her,
in the difference between people and groups can be seen

> the seeds of a tension that although painful, can and does
> produce growth, seeing in the differences of the other a much
> needed corrective to the biases of one's own social faction.
> The chaos of interdependence can be viewed as itself positive,
> as the fertile matrix of human creativity, leading to richer
> political and intellectual constructions as the insights and
> needs of various groups are fully taken into account.[10]

In every family, nation, or church, there will be some who
are 'difficult' or disruptive; not everyone will think the same. But
in the 'good enough' family, nation, or church, it will be possible
to live with difference, and manage the 'difficult' people. In its
decisions about women priests, the Church of England has not met
people's expectations that Christians should be able to do

everything harmoniously. However, perhaps it will prove to have been 'good enough' in allowing the strong feelings of anger to have expression, and in making provision for those who do not take the majority view. If a sense of belonging, either to the same denomination, or more broadly to the same Church of Christ, can survive despite the fights, the tantrums, and the tears, this is a true sign of being family.

The patience given by hope

Much of what is said about families today sounds a note of despair: that this time, society has reached depths from which it cannot emerge. I am not an optimist by nature, and therefore have found myself challenged time and again by the Christian virtue of hope. There are objective reasons why we need not sink into despair, as I showed earlier, but theologically too we have to maintain our belief both that human beings are capable of good, and that God is with us to sustain us whatever happens. Clearly, there is much evil in individuals – and if we are honest, we will recognize its presence in ourselves too. Yet if we believe people are made in the image of God, we have to hold on to the belief that there is also good within them, some spark which can be reached. For example, this is of the utmost importance in dealing with disruptive children. It can affect the way in which society deals with them, moving us in the direction of rehabilitation rather than revenge. Particularly if we ourselves have been victims of crime, we are likely to want to punish and be indignant at treatment which aims to reform, and appears to be rewarding the offence. Much of the indignation recently has been about treatment of young offenders; but it may be that they do need to be treated differently from adult criminals. Though those whose offence is severe will need custodial sentences, it is surely better to concentrate on helping offenders to go straight, rather than criminalizing them, and risking them persecuting society for years to come.

Equally, we have to recognize the power of structural evil, the way that sin is embedded in the world so that our best schemes often turn out badly. We have to acknowledge the way that groups and societies can be taken over by destructive impulses, so that people who may be both kind and moral in some circumstances can act brutally in others. But amidst all of that, Christians have to believe that hope, faith, and trust are not in vain. We live in a world that is often brutal, but in which it is always worth struggling for truth and justice, and where there are always, somewhere, glimpses of the divine. Good and evil, wheat and tares, grow together till the end of time. If we cannot eradicate evil, neither can anyone eradicate all that is good. What is required here is patience, a long-term view which refuses to be discouraged; 2 Corinthians 4 expresses some of this, and is relevant at a time when despair is easy to fall into: 'We are often troubled, but not crushed; sometimes in doubt, but never in despair . . . though badly hurt at times, we are not destroyed.'

The virtue of hope is needed also in looking at family itself. A number of people, including some within Christian feminism, are deeply critical of the family as a hopelessly patriarchal institution, damaging for children and adults alike. I want to argue that there is a future for family, and that there are ways in which families of different kinds can support and sustain us – despite the ways in which many go wrong. It is as unsatisfactory to give up on families because some are damaging, as to put them on a pedestal because some work well.

The kindness of compassion

Auden's ragged urchin had never heard of any world 'where one could weep because another wept'. No one had been compassionate towards him, and thus he could not feel compassion for others. Compassion has not yet gone out of existence, but it has become a fragile value in a society which promotes punitiveness and self-interest. Compassion is more easy to feel for those we love, although too often even in our close relationships we fail to stop and really understand what the other is going through. We may also find it easy to be compassionate towards those who come into our lives through the media, victims whom we can identify with – although it helps if the victim is a lovable and innocent child. Concern for victims of crime, disaster, or misfortune is important; that it emerges so strongly and so often is a sign of hope. Yet Christians have to go beyond this with their compassion, to show it to those who are unattractive, offenders, those who have contributed to their own hurts, those seen as outsiders. We are called to recognize not only that a victim is our neighbour, but that an offender is too. We are called to find our neighbour in those with whom we would prefer to have no dealings, and for the Church today this must include those whose lifestyles it regards as sinful.

We have to ask whether our attitudes and actions truly mediate God's love, for Oppenheimer's warning – that if we have ended up with legalism and moral censure we must have got it wrong – has to be heeded. There will always be the accusation that this is being weak and not judgemental enough, but this is precisely one of the charges that Jesus faced. His strongest condemnation was reserved for those religious leaders who laid heavy burdens on other people's shoulders. This is extremely difficult if we believe that there is a crisis in society caused by a failure to hold a firm line – and I shall say something about this later. None the less, we cannot evade our responsibility to allow people to encounter God, and perhaps to leave it to God to challenge them if that is what they need. As Walrond-Skinner remarks, this approach

> requires of us an inner conversion of attitude and spirit whereby we set aside our defensive legalism and fear, and engage with 'what is' rather than what we think 'ought to be'. It means a continuous effort to foster the spiritual disciplines of charity, faithfulness and hope, that we may perceive in the relationships of others the unique possibilities for them, which, with God's grace, will lead them to abundant life.[11]

Compassion is sometimes regarded as weak, being sorry for people who don't deserve it. Yet it is a hard-edged value – requiring us to take some hard decisions at times, as well as opening our hearts to others. Its opposite in this context is not so much judgementalism as carelessness. Not to have compassion is not to care what becomes of others, and that is something Christians can never accept.

The goodness that is integrity

Alasdair MacIntyre's book *After Virtue* suggests our age is comparable to the end of the Roman Empire, when the dark ages set in, and morality was disintegrating. In that situation, he says, it was the communities of faith which kept alive morality and civility. The pressing need now for MacIntyre is for local forms of community within which civility and morality can be sustained in the dark ages we are now in. This language echoes that of Christians who want to cut themselves off from a godless world in order to cultivate true religion, though this does not seem to be what MacIntyre intends. That sectarian approach must be avoided, for not only are Christians members of one humanity created by God, we also need to hear the challenges with which society confronts us. We are in danger if we see our own community as the only place where truth can be found.

Robin Gill's interpretation of the role of moral communities offers a way forward. Gill describes the way in which the key value of 'goodness beyond self-interest' is generated and nurtured in religious communities. This happens not because those within such communities are especially good, though he notes that religious affiliation is a good indicator of whether people will be involved in voluntary work and caring. Rather, religious communities carry such values through their stories, scriptures, rituals, and liturgies, even when this is not obvious to, or even always followed by, their adherents. Other communities can have strong moral beliefs, but it is the religious ones such as Judaism, Christianity, and Islam which encourage their adherents to look beyond their own interests, and which through worship offer an encounter with a God who cares and encourages them to care. The moral values which are 'carried' by religious communities spill out and become embedded in the rest of society, where their religious origin is often overlooked. He concludes that 'these values may finally make full sense if these roots are once again included within their meaning in our society.'[12]

This is a valuable perspective, although we also need to take account of the psychological reasons why people care 'beyond self-interest'. Some people devote themselves to others because they have grown up always striving to please demanding parents, and they seek activity in adult life which keeps them in this role. Such people may be more often found in religious communities, and may speak in overtly Christian terms about what they do. But it may be that even without religious values in society, there will still be people who need to care as a result of their own internal reasons. If this seems to deny spiritual motivation, it does not need to. If God can bring out of the distortions of family life people who contribute creatively to society, that is a cause for rejoicing – and may be one way in which 'goodness beyond self-interest' survives in 'dark ages'.

The Church's task for Gill is not to make pronouncements about moral positions, but rather to concentrate on living out moral values, like faithfulness, responsibility and caring.[13] Some of those outside the Church call on it to make moral pronouncements and to judge people's behaviour, without in any way wanting to be part of it themselves. By contrast, those who are drawn from outside into the Church often speak of responding to feeling loved and valued, welcomed into a community. This can happen where Christians welcome others into their own homes as well as in church buildings. A Church premised upon judgement will lose the people who at present come to it because they can catch a glimpse of God's affirming love. If they feel they will be criticized and judged, they will turn their back. Such a Church may be left feeling that it holds the high moral ground, but it is those outside who have paid the price.

Denise Carmody follows a similar line in her thoughtful reflection on feminist ethics, proclaiming that despite all its many imperfections, the Church is essential for human hope:

> simply by being visible the followers of Jesus who comprise the Church keep present in history the good news of the Reign of God. . . . If the Church merely exists, through the celebration of Christian Word and Sacrament, then the world can know that there is a community of salvation. If there is a community of salvation, then women and men can find a human, social place where a story powerful enough to heal their threatened imaginations, to cure their nearly mortally wounded spirits, sings praise to God without cease.[14]

The Church can try to foster its own integrity, to be a place where 'promises are kept'. 'If we say that we have no sin, we deceive ourselves', said the Book of Common Prayer, but admitting our weakness and failure as a Church is a sign of integrity. Better that, than pretending hypocritically that we can stand over against the rest of the world by judging its behaviour from a position of moral superiority. Our attempts to live by gospel values may not succeed very often, but we will be committed to trying, to insisting that these are the values which matter for ourselves and for our world. It has been shown that the most effective way in which parents teach values to their children is through modelling them, trying to live by them and acknowledging when they fail. It is surely important that the Church pays attention to what values our behaviour really holds out. How far do we show the love of God to each other and to those who are our neighbours? 'See how those Christians love one another!' is more often said today with sarcasm. Yet in our worship, we hear again and again of the loving forgiveness of God, and of our calling to share that love with others. All too often we are like the servant in Jesus' parable whose large debt was set aside, but who refused to forgo the much smaller amount owed him by another. We fail to pass on the loving freedom offered us in Christ, and instead concentrate on preserving our superiority and exclusivity.

It is not only the Church which needs to hold out these values, but if we wish to be a nation 'at ease with itself', then those in government and positions of influence also need to demonstrate that everybody matters. The divisions between rich and poor have widened, and when times are hard it is those who are poor who suffer, rather than those at the top.[15] There is no sense that we are all in this together, all having to suffer a little for the good of the nation. The scapegoating of particular groups in society, whether juvenile offenders or single parents, teachers, doctors, police, or clergy, contributes to the sense of a divided society in which each group has to fight for their own interests rather than being able to co-operate in a common cause. Social policy plays a part in allowing positive values to flourish, yet there is little sign that those in power in Britain have really taken that to heart.

A respect that means gentleness

'It takes mutual respect to make a family work', writes Kelly, 'not because parents and children are equals, but because they have an equal right to be respected.'[16] The theme of respect has run through this book, and it is essentially mutual respect, not something that must be given unconditionally to those in authority. I have floated the idea of respectful parenting, which respects the personhood of the child, and grants responsibility as appropriate for the child's growing maturity. Parents are 'respectable' in its literal sense if they are steady, responsible, trustworthy, and dependable, whether children are dependent or beginning to go their own way. Parents do have a certain amount of legal and moral authority, but need to keep in view the aim of enabling children to become responsible for themselves. Respect in this context is not the opposite of permissiveness, but of authoritarianism. It is not a question of making moral pronouncements which children must respect and obey, but of demonstrating positive values and guiding children as they grow and learn. Indeed, the degree of parental supervision has been shown to be a key factor in whether or not children become delinquent – children need to know that their parents care about what they do.

Respect for the father, held out as an important value by many Christians, needs to be rethought. Fathers, and mothers, are to be respected as people, and the scope of their authority recognized. But the value system which demands respect for fathers because they are men with a particular place in a hierarchical system no longer makes sense. Practically speaking, it prevents men from playing their proper role in their children's lives, for it keeps them at a distance. Theologically too, it does not belong in a Christian community where obedience to parents takes second place to obedience to God's calling. Elisabeth Fiorenza points to Jesus saying 'you shall call no-one "father" ', as a rejection of the patriarchal order of family life. Eisler shows how the challenge to the patriarchal pattern of family life has implications for the way the rest of society is run: ' "disrespect" for the male-dominated family in which the father's word is law, can be seen as a major threat to a system based on force-backed ranking.' She notes that 'the continued weakening of male control within the family is presented by many as part of a dangerous decline in the family. But the gradual erosion of the absolute authority of the father and husband was a critical prerequisite for the entire modern movement toward a more equalitarian and just society.'[17]

Commitment through faithfulness

It can be argued that all of us need to know that somebody is committed to us. We need to feel that there is someone we can depend on to be on our side, who will not reject us completely even if we behave badly. Without this, we become isolated and afraid. Perhaps a few people truly are happy to have no connections with anyone, but most of us need to feel that we matter to somebody. For Christians, some of this sense is found in the fact that we are valued by God, though we are created also to have connections with our fellow human beings. To want this kind of relationship is not inappropriate dependence, although that can be a danger, but one of the joyful possibilities of human existence. For this to happen requires commitment, but it can be a difficult value to maintain. How are we to continue being committed to another person whom we have ceased to love? It may help to see any emphasis on commitment or faithfulness as a reminder that we are not to be uncommitted or faithless. What is being rejected is the idea that commitments don't matter, that it is acceptable to promise one thing one day and go back on it the next. Keeping faith with a partner ought to mean being honest when a relationship begins to be unsatisfactory, and looking for ways to tackle the problems, rather than escaping into an alternative, adulterous relationship behind their back, and leaving them feeling profoundly betrayed. However, valuing commitment does not then mean insisting that people must never ever break their promises when circumstances have changed, and despite all their best endeavours, they cannot keep to their original intentions. There have to be ways of escaping from situations that have become impossible.

While the Church needs to offer care to those who face the breakdown of relationships, and ways of moving forward, it is imperative that we also do more to try to sustain commitment, to make it more possible for relationships to work. One way of doing this is through providing the opportunity for people to work on their relationships, both with partners and between parents and children. There are a number of schemes around which offer this, although I am not sure how well they have been evaluated. There is a need for more work that looks at couples whose relationships have survived difficult times, to assess what resources and other factors make this possible.[18] The emphasis in Britain has been more on sorting out the chaos when families collapse than on preventing the collapse in the first place. For example, readily available counselling services might help to prevent some marriage breakdown, but grants to Relate have been restricted.

Parent education has been defined as: 'a range of educational and supportive measures which help parents and prospective parents to understand themselves and their children and enhances the relationship between them'.[19] Pugh and De'Ath investigated the state of parent education and support in Britain in 1984. Though they found quite a lot going on, it was on rather a piecemeal basis, compared to the more formal organization of parent education in other countries. They point out that there are recommendations for parent education in government documents looking at such issues as violence in the family and teenage pregnancy, but this has not been matched with resources or put into a coherent policy. There are some problems with the concept and practice of parent education, which the authors discuss, and it clearly is not a panacea, or a substitute for addressing complex social problems. However, it is an idea worth promoting. As I noted earlier, there are also some recent attempts to work with young men, both offenders who have children, and other groups, who may have little idea of child development or of what being a good father entails.

Commitment, faithfulness, and duty can be harsh-sounding words. They seem to stand over against personal fulfilment and happiness, which we often see as requiring that we have our freedom to do as we please. We need to recapture their positive meanings. We do, after all, praise these values when we see them in other situations: the fire-fighter 'just doing their duty' to save someone's life; the employee who has served the same company for forty years; the commitment to each other of members of a team. To affirm these values is not to go back to suggesting that suffering is good for the soul, but seeing that people who voluntarily maintain commitment can find it rewarding. In addition, we need to develop the sense that individuals have a responsibility and duty to society and not just to the welfare of ourselves and those we love. I am interested to see how much the code of conduct drawn up by pupils and teachers at my daughter's Middle School emphasizes both the rights of children within the school and their role in the community. The notion that individual rights are always limited by the interests of others seems to be accepted – though how far it will be expressed in actual behaviour remains to be seen.

Limits – the value of self-control

Setting limits is important in family life. I have described the necessity for parents to provide a framework for children, in which some things are unacceptable, and this is essential if children are to learn self-control. There are two elements to this. The first concerns a child's safety, and parents are responsible for setting limits to ensure appropriate protection for children. This includes the process of civilizing them, so that they can fit in with the rest of society. The other element concerns values. A parent can be firm in their own beliefs, and will let a growing child know what these are, but cannot ensure that the child will hold the same values. Indeed, a parent may be led to question some of their values through their interaction with their offspring.

Can this be applied in relation to 'setting limits' in society? The Church is often expected to be a kind of parent, saying what is and is not acceptable in the world of private morality, and holding on to its own values in the face of rebellion from the rest of society. These values and limits may be out of date, or even harmful, but at least they set some sort of boundaries against which people can rebel. Without anything of this sort, people can feel lost. The Pope's 1993 encyclical *Veritatis Splendor* was praised by many for daring to hold out absolute values, to proclaim that there are such things as right and wrong. I have some sympathy with this view, but it has grave dangers if it takes no account of the content of what is being said. Many of those who react against the idea of the Church making pronouncements are objecting to the content of what is being said, rather than disputing the fact that there are some beliefs which are non-negotiable for Christians. The disagreement tends to be about what the 'absolutes' are, rather than whether there should be 'absolutes' in the first place. Thus someone who shies away from the idea of the Church pronouncing 'Cohabitation is wrong' might still call on it to say 'Exploitation is wrong'.

Most of us will agree that some limits need to be set, but both inside and outside the Church, we will not necessarily agree as to what they are. It is often said that we cannot reach any moral consensus in a pluralist society, but there probably are certain basic beliefs which the majority share, and which are enshrined in legislation about equality, or protection for children, or setting limits on some technologies. There will always be a minority who dissent, who will argue for racial discrimination or the exploitation of children, but it is usually still possible to get sufficient agreement about many moral issues, in order to allow action to be taken. The 'crisis in family values' is therefore not necessarily a crisis for all moral thinking. We are confused as a nation about morality in relationships, and how to deal with the fall-out from the variety of choices people are now making. There is also still confusion about the right way to deal with crime. But we should not despair of our ability to find some answers.

What we are unlikely to be able to do is to find universal answers to moral issues which can stand unexamined for ever. One of the problems for the churches is that many Christians would like to think we can do this. As Selby points out, 'Deep in the psychology of religious belief itself lies the quest for certainty and clarity which can easily turn into an arrogant or a punitive disposition.'[20] Christians seem especially likely to want certainty, to conquer doubt, and people can be drawn to religious groups precisely because they seem to offer certainties in a confusing world. But certainty is not what God promises. Christians will often go through periods when even God's existence seems in doubt, when the way forward seems unclear. Growing as a Christian requires that we think through our beliefs and actions; faith is not the conquering of doubt, but the ability to hold on to God when all seems lost.

Windfallen fruits

The Church's contribution to family issues is not so much to tell people where they have sinned, as to suggest the values which we believe will help people to form fulfilling relationships and which will undergird society. We do this not as an authoritative parent telling junior how to behave. Rather, the Church stands in relation to society as an elderly parent relates to adult children. The Church has, after all, helped to form society as we have it now, and Christian values are embedded in society. Our great age gives us some wisdom, though we are also continually learning from society and are challenged by it.

Gill speaks of values which are embedded, rooted, in society. I have been thinking about the image of windfallen fruits, on the ground, bruised, and often hard to find in the undergrowth. But they are there, accessible to us. Values of:

love	-	the interdependent community of love
joy	-	the joy of diversity
peace	-	the deep peace and order underlying chaos
patience	-	the patience given by hope
kindness	-	the kindness of compassion
goodness	-	the goodness that is integrity
gentleness	-	the respect which goes gently with others
faithfulness	-	the faithfulness expressed in commitment
self-control	-	the value of self-control; living within appropriate limits

Christians must judge any recital of family values by whether they spring from, are fruits of, the Spirit working in our lives. I do not claim that the ones I have set out here are the only ones needed, nor that these values alone are enough for the regeneration of society. Attention to justice must also be part of the equation. As Mary Grey says, 'mutuality-in-relating is about far more than improving one's personal relationships: it is about touching a deep source of relational energy in such a way as to liberate God's own passion for justice.'[21] But I offer this reconstruction of family values as an agenda for re-examining what we are doing as individuals, Church and society in relation to family issues.

The task facing us is of a different order from the simplistic solutions proposed when panic sets in. We find ourselves having to hold together individualism and community, realism and hope, integrity and compassion, and there is inevitably tension between them. We have to explore what upholding these values means in practice, faced with complex situations in families and society, and amid pressure to supply moralistic pronouncements. The call for the Church to maintain 'traditional family values' in a godless, amoral world is largely irrelevant, for it is based on inaccurate analysis of what this mixed-up world is really like, and on a very limited notion of what family values actually might be. Whatever the limitations of my own reconstruction of family values, my hope is that it might push us on to a different and more creative path, one which allows a few more of the fruits of the Spirit to be glimpsed in the undergrowth, and taken for our own.

Notes

1. H. Anderson, *The Family and Pastoral Care* (Philadelphia, Fortress Press, 1984), p. 79.

2. M. Grey, *Redeeming the Dream* (London, SPCK, 1989), p. 36.

3. I'm not sure where this phrase first originated, but I have heard several people use it.

4. B. Walsh, in *Third Way*, Summer 1992, pp. 28-9.

5. B. Ehrenreich and D. English, *For Her Own Good* (London, Pluto Press, 1979), p. 292.

6. H. Oppenheimer, *Marriage* (London, Mowbray, 1990), p. 4.

7. S. Walrond-Skinner, *The Fulcrum and the Fire* (London, Darton, Longman & Todd, 1993), p. 213.

8. J. Dominian, *Passionate and Compassionate Love* (London, Darton, Longman & Todd, 1991), pp. 219-20.

9. From 'In bread we bring you, Lord', by Kevin Nichols, *Hymns Old and New* (Kevin Mayhew Ltd).

10. S. Welch, *A Feminist Ethic of Risk* (Minneapolis, Fortress Press, 1990), p. 35.

11. Walrond-Skinner, *The Fulcrum and the Fire*, p. 215.

12. R. Gill, *Moral Communities* (Exeter, University of Exeter Press, 1992), p. 78.

13. *The Independent*, 24 December 1993.

14. D. Carmody, *Virtuous Woman* (New York, Orbis Books, 1992), p. 140-1.

15. Though those at the top may pay for it through increased crime and social unrest, as I noted in Chapter One.

16. M. Kelly, *The Mother's Almanac* (New York, Doubleday, 1989), p. 99.

17. E. Fiorenza, *In Memory of Her* (London, SCM Press, 1983); R. Eisler, *The Chalice and the Blade* (London, Pandora, 1990), pp. 129 and 161.

18. Interestingly, I heard of one study of married couples where simply being part of the study reduced the likelihood of divorce. Is it that knowing someone takes an interest in your marriage helps – and if so, are there lessons to be learnt?

19. G. Pugh and E. De'Ath, *The Needs of Parents* (London, Macmillan Education, 1984 (currently being updated)), p. 46.

20. P. Selby, *BeLonging* (London, SPCK, 1991), p. 58.

21. Grey, *Redeeming the Dream*, p. 104.

Index

General Synod, 57
General Synod BSR Working Party on the family, 7
gentleness, 132, 133, 206, 211
Gill, R., 33, 203
girls, 23, 24, 29, 92, 93, 98, 100, 101, 144, 160
goodness, 62, 122 - 126, 133, 186, 192, 203, 204, 211
government, 2, 12, 28, 31, 32, 36, 57, 62, 78, 82, 92, 96, 113, 118,
    122, 142, 150, 205, 208
grandparents, 41, 82, 158, 182
Grey, M., 29, 192, 194, 212

Health, 26, 33, 43, 45, 77, 78, 89, 90, 94, 96, 151, 182
homelessness, 35, 61
homosexuality, 76, 95;
    gay and lesbian, 60, 68, 75, 95, 96, 195
honouring parents, 133, 183, 186, 188
hope, 14, 17, 56, 85, 100, 124, 141, 197, 200 - 202, 204, 211, 212
household, 39, 40, 42, 43, 50, 55, 115, 180
housing, 24, 25, 68, 73, 78, 90, 92, 93, 103, 139

Individualism, 2, 27 - 29, 34, 77, 111, 149, 157, 166, 193, 194,
    212;
    individual rights, 26, 28, 149, 151, 193, 194, 196, 209
integrity, 35, 36, 57, 85, 203, 205, 211, 212
International Year of the Family, 25

Jesus, 42, 48, 50, 64, 83, 104 - 106, 120, 133, 163, 174, 180, 187,
    202, 204 - 206
joy, 74, 77, 133, 138, 187, 192, 195, 211
judgementalism, 202;
    condemnation, 60, 195, 202

Kindness, 115, 132 - 134, 192, 201, 211

Labour, 36, 44, 122
Left, the, Left-wing, 2, 13, 16, 18, 26, 121
legalism, 59, 202
limit setting, 58, 59, 116, 119, 121, 123, 152, 166, 179, 209 - 211